LEBRON

LEBRON

LIFE LESSONS
FROM THE KING

BRIAN BOONE

CASTLE POINT BOOKS
NEW YORK

To BWB, who lives for all things basketball,
but especially the Blazers. (Sorry, Bron.)

—*B.B.*

The Castle Point Books trademark is owned by Castle Point Publishing, LLC.
Castle Point books are published and distributed by St. Martin's Publishing Group.

ISBN 978-1-250-28215-6 (paper over board)
ISBN 978-1-250-28384-9 (ebook)

Design by Katie Jennings Campbell
Composition by Noora Cox
Illustrations by Gilang Bogy

Our books may be purchased in bulk for promotional, educational, or business use.

Please contact your local bookseller or the Macmillan Corporate and Premium
Sales Department at 1-800-221-7945, extension 5442,
or by email at MacmillanSpecialMarkets@macmillan.com.

First Edition: 2022

10 9 8 7 6 5 4

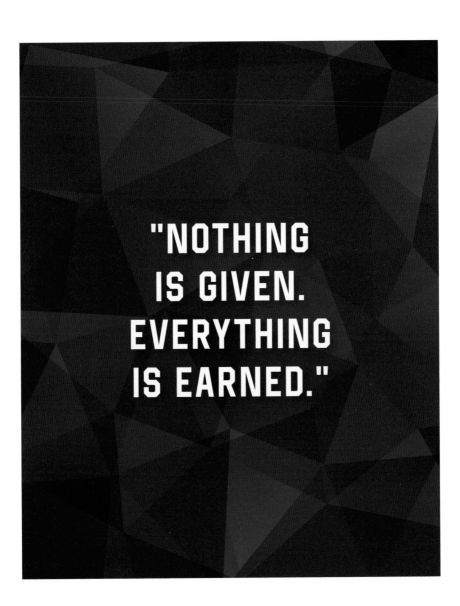

CONTENTS

INTRODUCTION 9

CHAPTER 1
Find What You Love 13

CHAPTER 2
Take Work Seriously ... 33

CHAPTER 3
Know What
Motivates You 45

CHAPTER 4
Learn from Others
and Let Others Learn
from You 61

CHAPTER 5
Wait for Your Moment ... 73

CHAPTER 6
Try New Things 93

CHAPTER 7
Get with Your Group 109

CHAPTER 8
Fight for
What's Right 121

I'M LEBRON JAMES 136
RESOURCES 139

INTRODUCTION

He's known by many nicknames: King James. The L Train. The Little Emperor. The Chosen One. The GOAT. But before all of those well-earned titles and all he's accomplished, basketball superstar LeBron James was merely, as he often reminds the world, "a kid from Akron." It's a telling insight into how LeBron sees himself and approaches his life's journey. He never forgets that he came from a humble background and got to where he is by setting goals, working hard, and remaining deeply motivated, even when (*especially* when) the road got rocky.

LeBron James stood out for his basketball talent early on. As a freshman at St. Vincent–St. Mary High School in Akron, Ohio, LeBron led his team to a perfect record and the first of multiple state titles. LeBron was named the best basketball player in Ohio for the first time as a sophomore, the first time an underclassman had ever landed the honor.

After receiving loads of national media attention for his remarkable abilities before he was even 18 years old, LeBron James was selected out of high school by the Cleveland Cavaliers with the first pick in the 2003 NBA draft. He would go on to win the Rookie of the Year Award, his first accolade in a pro career that would one day include four MVP awards, four NBA championships, and 18 All-Star team selections. He's even won three Olympic medals—two golds and a bronze—as a member of Team USA. LeBron has broken and set countless records, and has accomplished such remarkable feats on the court that he's regarded by many as the greatest basketball player who ever lived.

LeBron James pursues excellence. He never rests on his accomplishments. They only inspire him to reach the next level as a player and as a person. He developed his talents and skills until they were world class, and he's maintained them and improved upon them throughout his NBA career. From his expert shot-blocking to his tomahawk dunk to his stellar cross-court passing, LeBron has always had the power to put on a show. LeBron sets clear goals, lays out a plan on how to get there, and then acts on it. It's not that he hasn't struggled: He's failed and faced major disappointments, but he doesn't dwell on those failures. That's not where a champion puts his focus. LeBron puts all his energy into creating a lasting legacy, having changed the game—and the world around him—for the better.

LeBron has a path to greatness. He learned, even as a teenager, that he'd have to overcome every obstacle he encountered if he was going to be a success. For him, the key to becoming great lay in

"I'M GOING TO USE ALL MY TOOLS, MY GOD-GIVEN ABILITY, AND MAKE THE BEST LIFE I CAN WITH IT."

several different approaches. From his years as a teenage athlete to his time as a professional athlete and public figure, LeBron has never shied away from trying new things, learning from his triumphs and mistakes as he does so. He's also been patient with himself and with others, learning as much as he can by observing and working alongside them. LeBron fights for what he believes in, and he consistently defines and redefines what it is that motivates him on a deeper level. Even in a career that's pushing an improbable two decades, he's still giving his endeavors his all,

challenging himself (and the rest of us) to be the very best. When we examine his life and the choices he makes along the way, we can see the qualities that define a champion.

This book is about finding motivation, that hard-to-define, know-it-when-you-feel-it sense that makes you get up, go, and do it. LeBron James found it and never lost it, and he has used it to live out his wildest dreams. What LeBron learned about successfully reaching and exceeding goals is a blueprint that anyone with bold aspirations can follow.

FIND WHAT YOU LOVE

When a person discovers what it is they love to do, they will readily devote their lives to it, learning every aspect of it, studying its history, developing their skills, firing up their passions, and even helping it evolve into something better. To some, basketball is a game, a sport. But to others it is a calling, a passion, and a way of life. Those who choose to do it professionally, and who are talented and lucky enough to do so, find that it becomes a part of them. It makes them feel alive, like they have purpose, like playing that sport is what they were put on this planet to do.

LeBron's reason for being is not just to play basketball. Once he became one of the most successful and prominent athletes to ever pick up a ball, he expanded his goals. Not content to be one of the best (if not *the* best) to ever play hoops, he used his influence and gifts to open up his

HEART ON HIS SLEEVE

LeBron acknowledged his mother's importance by having her name tattooed on his right arm. It reminds him every day that she helped him grow into the person he is.

world and inspire others to do the same. LeBron James was lucky to discover what he wanted to do very early in life.

KEEP YOUR LOVED ONES CLOSE

LeBron James was once, as he likes to humbly refer to himself, a "kid from Akron." He was born on December 30, 1984, in the northeastern Ohio city of Akron. His mother, Gloria James, was 16 years old and still in high school when LeBron was born. She was living with her mother, Freda, and her brothers, Terry and Curt. LeBron's biological father wasn't a part of his life then or ever. He was an ex-convict who wanted no part of fatherhood, and for that reason LeBron hasn't pursued a relationship with him or talked much about him publicly. He relies on, and is devoted to, his doting mother.

"MY MOTHER IS MY EVERYTHING. ALWAYS HAS BEEN. ALWAYS WILL BE."

The lack of his biological father's presence and influence in his life, both as a child and beyond, had a lasting impact on LeBron. But instead of dwelling on the struggle of not having a father around, he used it to light a fire in himself. In a 2014 *GQ* profile, LeBron imagines what he'd say to his father if he could:

> *"I don't know you. I have no idea who you are. The fuel that I use today—you not being there—it's part of the reason I grew up to become who I am. It's part of the reason why I want to be hands-on with my endeavors. . . . So me in a position allowing people around me to grow, that maybe wouldn't have happened if I had two parents, two sisters, a dog, and a picket fence."*

For the first few years of his life, LeBron lived with his mother in his grandmother's home on Hickory Street in a low-income neighborhood where the unemployment and crime rates were high. All of the adults in his household, LeBron's grandmother, mother, and uncle worked low-wage jobs to keep themselves afloat, but it sometimes wasn't enough to pay the monthly bills. They barely scraped by, and sometimes they didn't get by. But the James household was an emotionally stable one, filled with love, support, and enthusiasm, particularly *for* little LeBron and *from* Freda James, the social glue of their family unit.

PLAY THROUGH DIFFICULTY

When LeBron was about one year old, Gloria James started to date a man named Eddie Jackson. A stellar former high school athlete, Eddie was the first person to share a love of sports with LeBron. He wanted LeBron to enjoy them as much as he did. Eddie Jackson was the most consistent and influential adult male role model in LeBron's early life. He was not perfect by any means, getting into trouble with the law on numerous occasions both before and after he came into LeBron's life, and serving time for it. But Eddie introduced LeBron to wrestling, and, in an even more monumental way, to basketball.

"I SAW DRUGS, GUNS, KILLINGS; IT WAS CRAZY."

The year that LeBron would turn three years old, Gloria and Eddie bought him a special Christmas present: a toy basketball hoop. That would prove a pivotal day in LeBron's life, as it marked the first time he'd be exposed to the game that would change and define his life. That Christmas consisted primarily of LeBron thrilled to play with his basketball hoop. As he remembers it, he spent the whole day shooting the ball, dunking the ball, and trying to see how high he could jump. Maybe he didn't know it yet, but on that day, LeBron got his first taste of the thing that would provide light and security for his family: basketball.

Strangely enough, on that same day, tragedy struck their home. Freda James, LeBron's grandmother, collapsed and died of a heart attack.

Not long after her death, the surviving members of the family could no longer afford the mortgage on the home. The bank foreclosed and turned it over to the city of Akron, which condemned it and tore it down. Terry and Curt went off on their own, and Eddie and Gloria parted ways, leaving LeBron and his mom to fend for themselves. They moved around a lot, bouncing from friends' to relatives' homes, sleeping on couches, eventually winding up in Elizabeth Park, a government-subsidized housing project that was run-down and well past its prime. One of the benefits: It had large open areas where LeBron could play and participate in sports with other kids. Unfortunately, a lot of illegal and dangerous activity occurred in those same areas, particularly drug deals and violent crime.

Eddie Jackson and Gloria James ended their relationship by the time LeBron was four years old, but Eddie stayed in LeBron's life as much as he could. He still refers to LeBron as his son, and during his first years as a basketball star, LeBron called Jackson "Dad" and would publicly thank him for his love, support, and influence. Gratitude came easily to LeBron. He was always aware that he was one of the lucky ones:

"My childhood was never great. We moved from place to place a lot. There were times when we had no definite place to stay. So, a basic level of security was not always there. Therefore, when you finally make it out, and you become who I am, you're humbled by the memories of those situations."

In the early days of his basketball career, and to some extent for his entire career, the fear of returning to those difficult years in Akron made him work harder to succeed.

BE READY TO ROLL

LeBron and Gloria James lived in Elizabeth Park off and on for six years, never really having a place to call their own. The year LeBron turned five years old, he and his mother moved seven times. Living this way taught him a lesson he kept with him for years: to be adaptable and to always be ready for what came next. "I just grabbed my little backpack, which held all the possessions I needed," LeBron said of this time in his life. "And said to myself what I always said to myself: It's time to roll." As they moved from place to place,

"I DON'T WANT TO GO BACK TO WHAT I'VE SEEN WHEN I WAS SEVEN, EIGHT, NINE YEARS OLD."

"I THINK THE REASON WHY I'M THE PERSON WHO I AM TODAY IS BECAUSE I WENT THROUGH THOSE TOUGH TIMES WHEN I WAS YOUNGER."

BUT FIRST, FOOTBALL

LeBron was a better football player than a basketball player in fourth grade. He played running back and defensive end for his youth team. The first handoff he took for the East Dragons ended in an 80-yard touchdown.

mother and son often depended upon the assistance of friends and community members. That's something else that LeBron would never forget, and he knew that when he was able to, he would pay back the goodwill shown to him by the people around him and the community of Akron.

The lack of stability in his home life was a source of stress for young LeBron, and his will and drive to succeed in school suffered. In his early elementary school years, he missed long stretches, preferring to stay home and play rather than attend classes. That all changed when a youth sports coach named Bruce Kelker took an interest in LeBron. He noticed LeBron's athletic build and height (already 5 feet 5 inches tall in fourth grade) and encouraged him to try out for the

East Dragons football team. From that moment on, LeBron continued on a sports trajectory.

LeBron looks back on this part of his life as the true turning point:

"I played football for a team called the East Dragons on the east side of town. We only had six regular season games. And six games I played tailback and I had 18 touchdowns in six games. That's when I knew I had some athletic ability."

When LeBron was in the fourth grade, his favorite part of the day, and his life at the time, was playing football. The assistant football coach, Frankie Walker Sr., saw tremendous promise in LeBron, but he also recognized that the child's scattered and stressful home life was not the ideal environment to provide the focus and stability that he needed. So, Walker devised a generous solution: He invited LeBron to live with him, his wife, and their three children during the school week. He'd spend time with his mother on the weekends.

The Walkers provided stability, structure, routines, and consistency for him in a way he hadn't experienced. The Walkers treated him like one of their own children, expecting him to contribute to the household chores while also celebrating his birthday, holidays, and personal accomplishments:

> *"It was like a new beginning for me. When I moved in with the Walkers, I went from missing 87 days my fourth-grade year to zero days in fifth grade. I love them. They are like my family. I wouldn't be here without them."*

In addition to helping raise LeBron and fostering the child's appetite for football, Walker also fostered LeBron's interest in basketball. He installed a hoop in his driveway so LeBron could practice, then signed him up to play in a recreational league at the Summit Lake Community Center, an inner-city, youth-oriented activity hall where Walker coached basketball.

Walker was LeBron's first basketball teacher and coach. While instructing him in the basics of the game, Walker realized that this developing player was a quick study. He had the kind of natural athletic ability that, if properly cultivated, could take LeBron very far.

LeBron's first experience on a basketball team was playing for Walker's fourth-grade team. When LeBron wasn't playing games, he was practicing at Walker's home and at the community center, perfecting his stroke by taking shots from every point on the court. LeBron absorbed so much knowledge so quickly, and developed his mental acuity for basketball so rapidly, that when he was in the fifth grade, Walker made LeBron a coach for the fourth-grade team. At age 10, LeBron started to fill

"IF YOU'VE GOT
THE DRIVE,
THE DISCIPLINE,
AND THE RESOLVE
TO DO WHAT IT
TAKES TO MAKE
YOURSELF GREAT,
THEN THE REWARDS
ARE ENDLESS."

as much of his life as possible with basketball, because it was emerging as his true passion. With his developing physical skills and a progressively deeper mental grasp on the game, he would soon be unstoppable.

In the fifth grade, LeBron joined the Northeast Shooting Stars, a team in the large, national Amateur Athletic Union (AAU) sports league, coached by Dru Joyce II. He joined a junior superteam already in the making, playing alongside rising stars Sian Cotton, Willie McGee, and Dru Joyce III. The four basketball stars called themselves the "Fabulous Four," forging a strong bond that would last for years, providing LeBron with an inner circle of fellow players who understood him. He'd rely on this group for support, both on and off the court, for decades.

> *"You know, my family and friends have never been yes-men: 'Yes, you're doing the right thing, you're always right.' No, they tell me when I'm wrong, and that's why I've been able to stay who I am and stay humble."*

LOVE BRINGS FOCUS

A star of the AAU circuit in junior high, LeBron, along with the rest of the Fabulous Four, was recruited to attend St. Vincent–St. Mary High School, a small, private parochial school in Akron, where renowned local coach Keith Dambrot was setting up a new program. Together, LeBron and friends had one goal: to win the first state championship title for the school, which was primarily known for its rigorous academics. Because of its high standards—90 percent of graduates went on to attend college—academic failure was not an option. To continue pursuing the thing he loved, basketball, LeBron had no choice but to study hard and work hard at his schoolwork and at athletics.

LeBron was also a star wide receiver for the St. Vincent–St. Mary Fighting Irish football team. In one fruitful season, LeBron led his team to the Ohio state semifinals, catching 62 passes and amassing 1,200 yards. In a playoff game, he broke a finger. His mother, who had worried he'd get hurt from the beginning, forbade him to play football after that and only allowed him to play basketball.

With the broken finger barely slowing him down and one sport as his focus, LeBron fully embraced his basketball destiny at St. Vincent–St. Mary. Having added hard work and stellar effort to a talent that was already there, he'd found a recipe for unstoppable success. Coaches commended LeBron not just for his scoring ability, but for how he could expertly rebound, pass, and defend, all at the skill level of an older high school or college player. In his freshman year, with LeBron leading the team as the starting point guard and top scorer, the Fighting Irish went undefeated through the regular season and playoffs. In the Ohio state championship game, LeBron scored 25 points, and St. Vincent–St. Mary beat the Greeneview Rams of Jamestown, Ohio. The Fab Four made good on their promise to themselves and their school to win a state title at the first opportunity possible.

KEEP AT IT

Already looming large at 6 feet 4 inches tall, LeBron grew three inches the summer after his freshman year of high school. That extra height made him even more dominant on the court. In his sophomore season, St. Vincent–St. Mary amassed a 27–1 record. Undeterred, and driven to win, play, and enjoy basketball, his team again won the Ohio state title. LeBron was named the postseason tournament's most valuable player. Additionally, he was named first team All Ohio and "Mr. Basketball," the best player in the state. He was the first sophomore to ever earn that honor.

CELEBRITY CAME EARLY

USA Today featured LeBron on its list of the best high school basketball players in the country in 2002, when he was only 16 years old.

In his junior year, LeBron, driven by the accolades as much as the joy of the game, got even better, averaging 29 points a game and once again was named Ohio's Mr. Basketball and one of *USA Today*'s national best. In the 2001–02 season, LeBron was also named Gatorade's National Boys Basketball Player of the Year. However, he also experienced his first real on-court disappointment that year. St. Vincent–St. Mary lost the state title game to Roger Bacon High School from Cincinnati. It was only the second loss of his high school career. Nevertheless, he took it in stride and moved on because he knew his future was bright.

In February 2002, he appeared on the cover of *Sports Illustrated*, heralded as "The Chosen One." NBA coach and executive Danny Ainge was quoted in the magazine saying that LeBron could be drafted by a team with the No. 1 pick right then—and he was still in high school.

DON'T GIVE UP

LeBron loved basketball so much that in addition to his high-profile high school games, he continued playing for an AAU squad. During a 2002 AAU game, he came up hard against an opposing defender and landed on his non-shooting hand. Fortunately, the injury was a wrist sprain; a serious break requiring surgery or long-term rehab could have derailed everything. LeBron knew he had to get himself back in shape as quickly as possible or risk losing opportunities, so he practiced

STAT ⚡ **LeBron James' individual stats as a high school player were off the charts. As a freshman, he averaged 21 points a game, which he increased to 25.2 as a sophomore. After resisting the idea to enter the 2002 NBA draft at age 17, LeBron returned for his senior year and averaged 31.6 points and 9.6 rebounds per game.**

IN GOOD COMPANY

The 2003 NBA draft was one of the most stacked drafts in league history. Four out of the first five selections became NBA all-time greats: LeBron, Carmelo Anthony, Chris Bosh, and Dwyane Wade.

and played when he could despite his injury. In his senior year, having stayed the course, risen to new heights, and proving that he wasn't a flash in the pan, LeBron once again won a state title and was named Mr. Basketball of Ohio.

What was next for LeBron James? Bigger basketball venues. While he entertained offers from major college basketball programs during high school, LeBron opted to forgo college and instead declared his eligibility for the 2003 NBA draft. He wanted to play basketball professionally, and he felt he had the skills and passion to make his debut in the world's most prestigious league. In June 2003, LeBron James was the first selection in the NBA draft. In a twist of good luck for everyone involved, that pick belonged to the Cleveland Cavaliers,

who played just 30 miles from LeBron's hometown. The kid from Akron was on his way to Cleveland—and much bigger things.

STICK TO YOUR DECISIONS

A big part of doing what you love is doing what's right for *you*. For LeBron James, basketball and winning at basketball always felt right to him, and this helped guide all of his decisions.

The usual path for high school basketball standouts starts with heavy recruitment by top college basketball programs. The athletes take their pick, play at that level for one to four years, then officially declare themselves eligible for the NBA draft, and (hopefully) go pro. LeBron boasted such tremendous talent as a high school athlete that he was able to play the course a little

"MY DREAM HAS BECOME A REALITY, AND IT'S THE BEST FEELING I'VE EVER HAD."

differently. Choosing the road less traveled, he made himself open for the NBA draft in April 2003, before graduating from high school. He decided to skip college altogether and go straight to the professional level, something very few basketball players attempt. Later in his career, he explained his thinking. College players weren't allowed to sign endorsement deals and couldn't profit from their success the way NBA players could. He wanted financial security for himself and his mom.

Making hard decisions, and sticking to them, is a recurring theme in the life and basketball career of LeBron James. Much later in his career, he went against the grain yet again and made a widely critiqued decision—

all because he wanted to follow his gut. In July 2010, after seven seasons with the Cleveland Cavaliers, LeBron became an unrestricted free agent. He had fulfilled his contract and was able to sign with an NBA team of his choice. Because he was already a superstar, many teams were eager to bring him to their cities, and owners, executives, coaches, and players publicly tried to woo LeBron. (Other stars hesitated to sign extensions or new contracts until they knew where LeBron was going, on the off chance that they could play alongside him.) LeBron showed up at a Cleveland office building with representatives from several high-profile franchises, including the Los Angeles Clippers, Chicago Bulls, New Jersey Nets, and New York Knicks, to hear their offers.

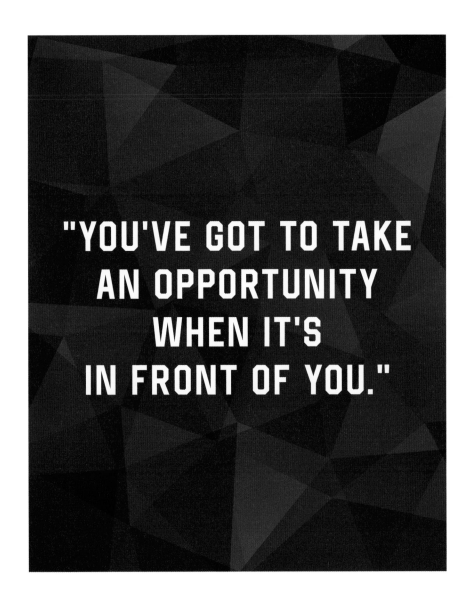

"YOU'VE GOT TO TAKE AN OPPORTUNITY WHEN IT'S IN FRONT OF YOU."

He carefully weighed the pros and cons of playing for each team interested in him, and decided that the best place for him was the Miami Heat. He'd been frustrated by the fruitless struggle to win a championship in Cleveland, so he made the difficult decision to leave:

"I'm going to take my talents to South Beach and join the Miami Heat. I feel like it's going to give me the best opportunity to win and to win for multiple years, and not only just to win in the regular season or just to win five games in a row or three games in a row, I want to be able to win championships. And I feel like I can compete down there."

Some of the other teams wanted to use LeBron to start building a roster that could eventually contend for a championship. But with Miami, he saw a winning culture already in place, with a franchise full of people who knew how to earn titles, like executive Pat Riley, and head coach Erik Spoelstra.

His fans in Cleveland were outraged, feeling that their homegrown superstar was abandoning them to "chase a ring" with a proven squad rather than continue striving in Cleveland. But LeBron didn't want to

"THE GAME ALWAYS GIVES BACK TO PEOPLE THAT ARE TRUE TO THE GAME. I'VE WATCHED IT."

"I ALWAYS SAY, DECISIONS I MAKE, I LIVE WITH THEM."

wonder *what if* and shy away from taking a chance on a new team. In the end, the decision set him on the path and helped him accomplish his goal. In Miami, he learned how to be a champion from other champions, a skill he would eventually bring back to Cleveland.

LIFE LESSONS FROM THE KING

- HAVE A SUPPORT SYSTEM, AND HOLD ON TO IT.
- TRY SOMETHING NEW AND YOU MIGHT DISCOVER A FOREVER PASSION.
- YOU CAN NEVER TRY TOO HARD OR PRACTICE TOO MUCH.
- STAND BY YOUR DECISIONS.

TAKE WORK
SERIOUSLY

Success isn't guaranteed, even for someone with astounding, once-in-a-generation talent who has numerous opportunities to showcase those gifts as early, and as often, and for as long as possible. True achievement takes a lot of effort. To truly make a mark on the world, to truly become the best that's ever been at whatever it is you do, you have to put in the work.

LeBron James is heralded by many as the greatest basketball player of all time, but that wasn't guaranteed from the first time he put on an NBA uniform, or even a high school or AAU uniform. Coaches and relatives recognized some raw athletic ability, and he was lucky enough to reach a height of 6 feet 8 inches while still in high school. From there, LeBron had to take the reins. He had to get good enough at basketball to make himself known, and then prove himself worthy of the world's preeminent basketball league. Even when he was in the NBA, LeBron understood that he had to put in the legwork, practicing, studying, and perfecting the physical and mental elements of the game, so that he could one day make an All-Star team or win a championship.

FOCUS ON IMPROVEMENT

LeBron's success came from knowing that even when you lose, you win, if in the process you learn something. Whether it was mental work or physical work, he was always ready to do it differently or better depending on what the situation demanded of him. He was a stellar point guard for his AAU and high school basketball teams. He knew he'd have to prove his mettle when he entered the NBA.

When LeBron suited up for the Cleveland Cavaliers in 2003, he was a rookie who had to live up to a lot of hype. At 19, he'd already earned comparisons to Michael Jordan for his strength, skill, and versatility. In his first season, LeBron (who was already being referred to as "King James" and "The Chosen One") did not disappoint. He averaged 5.9 assists and 5.5 rebounds. His shooting, though, left some room for improvement. Paul Silas, his head coach, was impressed by his young player's maturity and commitment to improving. Over the course of the season, he watched his No. 1 pick self-assess and grow:

"The one thing he needed to work on was his outside shooting, and he worked on that. I think it really helped that I would have the team take 100 shots every practice and 25 or 30 of those were 3-pointers. But he had a work ethic, and he got better."

LeBron's shooting average was 41.7 percent in his first season, including 29.0 percent on 3-pointers. Just one season later, he'd improved both of those stats: 47.2 percent and 35.1 percent on 3-pointers. Those numbers would continue to rise as the star player evolved into a true legend:

"I try to get better each and every season, try to get better at every aspect of the game, step outside

"I CAN'T CHEAT THE GAME. YOU ONLY HAVE SO LONG TO PLAY THIS GAME AT A HIGH LEVEL, AND I WANT TO DO MY PART TO MAKE SURE I'M STILL PROGRESSING."

my comfort zone. [I focus on] things that I may not have done the year before, that I wasn't comfortable with, and get better at it, and be the best player I can be."

LeBron kept at it and made enough of an impression to be considered for, and ultimately get a spot on, the USA Men's Basketball 2004 Olympic team. He continued his ascent in the NBA and grew into a player who could play just about any position, and one who could adapt and self-correct in a way that made him nearly unstoppable.

STAT ⚡ In his first three seasons with the Cavs, LeBron's field goal percentage improved from 41.7 to 47.2 to 48.0. Apart from a slight dip in 2006–07, he managed to keep improving his shooting accuracy every year for the next seven years. By the 2013–14 season, his field goal percentage was up to 56.7.

GO BIG OR GO HOME

Champions like LeBron keep elevating themselves and changing the goal posts: Each achievement opens a new door and inspires loftier goals. Only 60 players are drafted into the NBA each year, and LeBron was at the top of his class (a stellar group in 2003 that included Dwyane Wade and Carmelo Anthony). Only a handful of those 60 make a demonstrable contribution to the NBA or go on to be superstars, All-Stars, or champions. LeBron James knew he could get further than most NBA draft picks. He was hungry to show the world, and himself, how much he could accomplish.

In LeBron's first year with the Cleveland Cavaliers, the team's record improved significantly from a dismal 17-65 to 35-47. It still wasn't enough to make the playoffs, nor would a 42-40 finish the next year, but that progress proved his worth and sent a message that he was more than just hype.

LeBron's rookie year was the only season in his career when he didn't make an All-Star team, though it was mainly because rookies aren't typically named to that elite club. He did, however, earn the NBA's Rookie of the Year award. At 19, he set a record as the youngest player to ever achieve that honor. He's since been named to 18 All-Star teams, demonstrating his unrelenting determination and the longevity of his success on the court.

After his standout rookie campaign, LeBron began to set even loftier goals: He wanted to be better than everyone around him (rookies and All-Stars alike), and he was determined to one day win an NBA title.

STAT ⚡ **LeBron came into the league with a strong start. He averaged 20.9 points as a rookie. In comparison, most first-year players don't break double digits. Kevin Garnett averaged 10.4 points in his rookie year, while Kobe Bryant averaged 7.6 points.**

"COMMITMENT IS A BIG PART OF WHAT I AM AND WHAT I BELIEVE."

BIG MONEY

LeBron is still one of the top 10 highest-paid basketball players in the NBA, and that's just his salary. His endorsement deals bring in over $100 million annually. In 2021, LeBron set a record for being the first active NBA player to earn $1 billion over the course of his career, an astonishing figure that includes salary, endorsements, merchandise, licensing, and media.

KNOW YOUR WORTH

From the time he was a rookie, LeBron took basketball seriously and knew it could provide a secure life for him, his mom, and his future family. He didn't squander his salary on fancy cars and big houses. He took a more calculated approach. When he looked at the future, he saw a career that went way beyond basketball:

> *"In the next 15 or 20 years, I hope I'll be the richest man in the world. That's one of my goals. I want to be a billionaire. I want to get to a position where generation on generation don't have to worry about anything. I don't want family members from my kids or my son's kids to have to worry. And I can't do that now just playing basketball."*

This ambitious outlook is why LeBron James is still an elite professional athlete and a business mogul even as he nears age 40, when basketball players usually think about retiring (or have already done so). He's been using his vision and his competitive nature to knock down barriers and build a successful brand ever since. And he's not about to give up after having come all this way from the housing projects and high school basketball scene in Akron, Ohio.

WORK HARDER THAN EVERYONE ELSE

If every day is founded on a mindset of greatness, then greatness happens. LeBron never fails to try as hard as he can on a daily basis, often raising the bar for himself and his teams.

"THERE IS A LOT OF PRESSURE PUT ON ME, BUT I DON'T PUT A LOT OF PRESSURE ON MYSELF. I FEEL IF I PLAY MY GAME, IT WILL TAKE CARE OF ITSELF."

"I KNOW THERE IS SOMEONE, SOMEWHERE, TRYING TO TAKE MY SPOT."

With family, teammates, coaches, and fans—even opposing ones—relying on him, there's no option to rest. His own high standards prevent him from easing the pressure. When reflecting on the work he put in with the Miami Heat when he was striving for a title, he admits that, in general, he doesn't feel content unless he's giving it his all:

"I show up to work, and I don't leave until I feel like I was as great as I was. Do you always become successful at it? Are you always going to win? No, it doesn't happen like that. But you're able to sleep a little bit better at night when you know you've punched the clock."

LeBron's work ethic is up there with the likes of Kobe Bryant, and other players and coaches have taken notice. Lance Stephenson witnessed it firsthand when he played with LeBron on the Los Angeles Lakers: "I watched LeBron work out. Super professional. First one on the plane, first one at the meetings, first one at the workout, first one in the gym, he's first in everything."

It's difficult to give the game your all when an injury or illness strikes, but LeBron doesn't know any other way. When the Cavaliers were scheduled to hit the road for a game against the Chicago Bulls in 2017, LeBron came down with a nasty case of the flu. Despite his physical condition, he dug deep, suited up, and still played like a champion: He scored 31 points on 12-of-21 shooting from the field, eight rebounds, and seven assists. After the game, he told reporters that he did it for the fans:

"I've been fortunate to have packed houses every night I go on the floor. . . . I don't want them to leave disappointed. So once the lights turn on and the fans come in and the popcorn starts popping, I'll be ready to go."

But fans or no fans, it's hard to imagine LeBron backing down from any challenge.

He makes striving a part of everyday life, so much so that the world is accustomed to LeBron putting on an incredible performance night after night, year after year. He doesn't rest on his substantial achievements or take his foot off the gas. He's hungry for more, always looking for the next challenge, the next mountain to scale.

LIFE LESSONS FROM THE KING

- WORK WITH A PURPOSE, AND THE JOURNEY WILL LEAD TO SUCCESS.
- DREAM BIG, BUT PLAN BIG ON YOUR WAY TO YOUR DREAMS.
- ONCE YOU MEET YOUR GOALS, SET HIGHER ONES AND KEEP STRIVING.
- STAY PERSISTENT IN YOUR EFFORTS.

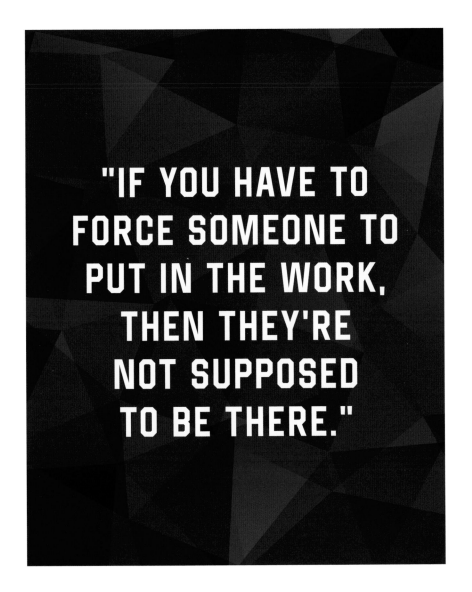

"IF YOU HAVE TO FORCE SOMEONE TO PUT IN THE WORK, THEN THEY'RE NOT SUPPOSED TO BE THERE."

KNOW WHAT MOTIVATES YOU

Over the course of his long, productive, and remarkably successful NBA career, LeBron James has managed to be one of the most dominant players in the game by keeping in mind what matters most to him: making his fans proud, proving his critics wrong, and demonstrating to himself that he could do anything he set out to do. Knowing who and what he is fighting for helps him power through difficult challenges, clear his own path to success, and achieve things other basketball players only dreamed of achieving. He never loses sight of why he's working toward his goals, which makes him tenacious and, often, unbeatable.

BE YOURSELF

When LeBron was a high school basketball star, he wore number 23. He also wore it through his seven-year stint with the Cleveland Cavaliers. The 23 was a tribute to Chicago Bulls legend Michael Jordan, who wore that number

"THERE WILL NEVER BE ANOTHER MICHAEL JORDAN. YOU'LL DRIVE YOURSELF CRAZY TRYING TO BE THE NEXT MICHAEL JORDAN."

throughout his storied career. When LeBron moved to the Miami Heat in 2010, he felt that it was time for a new number. The reason: He didn't want to invite comparisons to Jordan, or be "the next" Jordan. LeBron wanted to be himself; LeBron wanted to be the first and only LeBron James. He wanted to free himself from the "Jordan vs. LeBron" debate, the ongoing argument among basketball fans and sportswriters over who is the "GOAT," or the greatest of all time. For LeBron, the comparison is pointless and harmful:

"I'm chasing what I can potentially do. And that's a goal I have for myself. At the end of the day, I can't rank myself where I want in NBA history; that's for everyone else to do. But I have the potential to be really good at this game."

FAMILY IS EVERYTHING

When LeBron eventually suited up for the Miami Heat, he made a change to his jersey number. He went from number 23 to number 6. The number 6 has personal significance, and it reminds him why and for whom he plays and works so hard. His son LeBron James Jr. was born on October 6, and his youngest son, Bryce, was born in June, the sixth month. The role of fatherhood had changed his perspective:

"I go home and see my son, and I forget about any mistake I ever made or the reason I'm upset. I get home and my son is smiling or he comes running to me. It has just made me grow as an individual and grow as a man."

Not only does LeBron think of his children every time he dons a jersey bearing the number 6, but he taps into his love for his family to train and play even harder. Prior to game 5 of the 2012 NBA Finals, LeBron delivered a pep talk to his teammates to get them fired up for the crucial contest. "If someone came to you right now and told you, 'If you don't win tonight, you won't see your family again,' how would you play?" LeBron asked them. Then he took it further: "Approach this game like your family is in danger. How bad do you want to see your family again?" Thinking of the high stakes of any challenge, or just considering why one works so hard, creates a fire and an urgency. For LeBron, it solidifies in his mind that losing is not even an option, which leads to a showing of intense, unmatched effort, night after night.

PROVE YOUR CRITICS WRONG

Criticism, particularly aggressive and outsized criticism on the part of fans, sports journalists, and industry pros, can be a powerful motivating force for an athlete who knows how to channel it. LeBron James knew how to channel it. Despite being one of the greatest NBA players of his era, he endures a great deal of criticism from naysayers who doubt his skills, and who go out of their way to critique elements of his game. Instead of taking offense or feeling hurt, LeBron lets that kind of commentary fuel him. When adversaries publicly question his talents or even his commitment to basketball, he proves how wrong they are by winning games and making them eat their words.

When LeBron announced in 2010 that he was leaving the Cleveland Cavaliers, his professional home for seven seasons, in favor of the Miami Heat, he did so via an ESPN special (produced by his own company) called "The Decision." He told sportscaster Jim Gray:

"This fall, I'm going to take my talents to South Beach and join the Miami Heat. I feel like it's going to give me the best opportunity to win and to win for multiple years, and not only just to win in the regular season."

LeBron was heavily criticized for "The Decision," which was described as self-indulgent, self-aggrandizing, and arrogant. His fans in Cleveland resented him and felt betrayed. They'd supported him for years, not just in his professional career but when he was a high school star, and now they felt abandoned. Many fans burned LeBron jerseys in public and in online videos. Cleveland Cavaliers owner Dan Gilbert posted an open letter to LeBron on the team website, calling him out for deserting his franchise and home region with the "bitterly disappointing" TV special. "I personally guarantee that the Cleveland Cavaliers will win an NBA championship before the self-titled former 'King' wins one," Gilbert wrote.

There's no question that this response was difficult for LeBron to bear. "It was unfortunate, because I believed in my heart that I had gave that city and that owner, at that point in time, everything that I had," he said in 2017. "Unfortunately, I felt like, at that point in time, as an organization, we could not bring in enough talent to help us get to what my vision was."

It was nothing personal toward Cleveland, the Cavaliers, or Gilbert. LeBron needed to serve his desire

STAT ⚡ In his first 17 seasons in the NBA, LeBron James finished in the top five of Most Valuable Player voting every year, an all-time record.

to capture an NBA title. Winning was his ultimate goal, and he was ready to use a critique like that from Gilbert to bolster his determination.

MONEY ISN'T EVERYTHING

In a professional career that's lasted nearly two decades, LeBron James has made a lot of money playing basketball. His salary earnings from NBA contracts have amassed him $387 million. That makes him one of the richest athletes in history and one of the wealthiest Americans under age 40. LeBron was also the league's highest-paid player in 2016–17, when he made $30.9 million for his unmatched skills.

While this is admittedly a lot of money, as the greatest basketball player on the planet, LeBron certainly could bring in more money on a season-to-season basis, but he takes a different approach:

"I have not had a full max deal yet. That doesn't matter to me; playing the game is what matters to me. That's the genuine side of this. It's about winning."

"A LOT OF PEOPLE SAY THEY WANT TO WIN, BUT THEY REALLY DON'T KNOW HOW [MUCH HARD WORK] IT TAKES, OR A LOT OF PEOPLE DON'T HAVE THE VISION."

"ALL THAT MATTERS
IS TO PLAY AT A
HIGH LEVEL AND DO
WHATEVER IT TAKES TO
HELP YOUR TEAM WIN."

A bigger paycheck hasn't mattered to LeBron as much as reaching his professional goals, so he sacrificed the paycheck to acquire titles. For the 2010–11 season, LeBron agreed to a deal with the Miami Heat that netted him $14.5 million. Keeping his salary far lower than his market value allowed his team to stay under the NBA's salary cap limitations, meaning the Heat had plenty of money in the bank to pursue top-level players to play alongside and support LeBron.

The team acquired All-Star Chris Bosh from Toronto, creating a jaw-droppingly talented trio with Bosh, LeBron, and team veteran Dwyane Wade. "The Big Three" won back-to-back championships for the Heat.

TENACIOUSLY PURSUE THE NEXT LEVEL

Instead of being insulted by the doubts and critique of others, LeBron took their words as a challenge and decided to play extra hard to show his naysayers that the only mistake would have been to stay in Cleveland when he knew Miami was a stepping-stone to success.

LeBron left the Cleveland Cavaliers for the Miami Heat in order to learn how to win at the highest level, playing alongside title-winning players and proven champions like Dwyane Wade and legendary coach and team executive Pat Riley. LeBron spent four seasons with the Miami Heat, playing his heart out. He led the Heat to the NBA Finals every season he played there, winning in 2012 and 2013, and being named the NBA Finals MVP on both occasions. The 2013 NBA Finals bore some especially dazzling LeBron performances. In game 1, he racked up a triple-double (double digits in points, rebounds, and assists), led the Heat in scoring five times (including his 37 points in the decisive game 7), pulled down the most rebounds four times, and amassed the most assists in four games.

LeBron James ultimately proved his critics wrong. In winning back-to-back titles with the Miami Heat, he showed that he possessed all of the skill, talent, and qualities necessary to earn an NBA championship. He showed that leaving Cleveland was the only way

"I PUT MY BLOOD, SWEAT, AND TEARS IN THE GAME. AND PEOPLE STILL WANT TO DOUBT WHAT I'M CAPABLE OF DOING."

he could reach his highest goal. He went to Miami to take his game to the next level, and he accomplished what he knew he could do.

HONOR YOUR COMMUNITY

In 2014, despite being positioned for even more success in Florida, and despite the criticism he knew he'd face, LeBron announced that he would return to the Cavaliers. Cleveland hadn't enjoyed a major sports title in more than 50 years. LeBron decided that he would deliver a championship, a winning feeling, and a sense of pride to his birthplace. In an interview with

Sports Illustrated, he did his best to explain the move home:

> *"When I left Cleveland, I was on a mission. I was seeking championships, and we won two. But Miami already knew that feeling. Our city hasn't had that feeling in a long, long, long time. What's most important for me is bringing one trophy back to northeast Ohio."*

Aside from wanting to deliver a win to his home state, he was also feeling a pull to raise his family there. At the time, he already had two sons, and his wife, Savannah, was pregnant with a girl. Some part of him always wanted to raise his kids there:

"I started thinking about what it would be like to raise a family in my hometown. I looked at other teams, but I wasn't going to leave Miami for anywhere except Cleveland. The more time passed, the more it felt right. This is what makes me happy."

LeBron signed a two-year deal with the Cleveland Cavaliers, where, similar to what he'd done with the Heat, he took a central role on a team of iconic players. With LeBron back in the good graces of owner Dan Gilbert, and with Kyrie Irving and Kevin Love there to add their star power, the Cavs were in a position to dominate. In his first season back in Cleveland (2014–15), LeBron led the Cavaliers to the NBA Finals. They eventually lost to the Golden State Warriors, but it was a great start.

During the series, LeBron dropped reporters a clue about the "other motivation" that fueled him to win, but he would only reveal it if the Cavs won. The secret stayed safe with LeBron throughout the 2015–16 season, until the Cavs were once again matched up with the Golden State Warriors in the NBA Finals. The Warriors had finished the regular season with a record-setting 73 wins in 82 games, led by Most Valuable Player Steph Curry. This would not be easy.

DON'T BE AFRAID OF CHANGE

In the 2016 NBA Finals, the Warriors jumped out to a 3-1 lead in the best-of-seven series. If LeBron's Cavaliers lost one more game, the Warriors would win a second consecutive NBA title. This only served to motivate LeBron to play harder. Nobody had ever come back from a 3-1 deficit to win the NBA Finals, but LeBron did not give up. With his back against the wall, he put on one of the most impressive and dominant basketball performances in NBA history and brought the Cavs back from the brink.

In game 5, LeBron had 41 points and 16 rebounds, lifting the Cavaliers to victory. In game 6, he scored 41 points again, and the Cavs took that

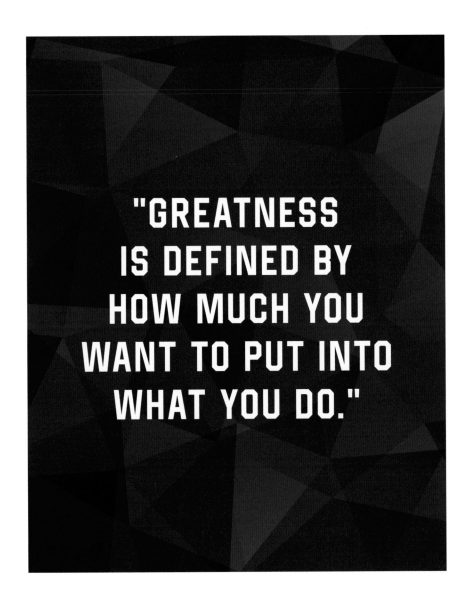

"GREATNESS IS DEFINED BY HOW MUCH YOU WANT TO PUT INTO WHAT YOU DO."

"THERE'S THAT MOMENT
EVERY MORNING
WHEN YOU LOOK
IN THE MIRROR:
ARE YOU COMMITTED,
OR ARE YOU NOT?"

game, too. With another 27 points in the decisive seventh game, LeBron's Cavs won by four points, capturing the title and finally bestowing a long-awaited championship on Cleveland. LeBron made the people of northeast Ohio feel like champions again, instilling pride in sports fans who hadn't enjoyed that championship feeling since the mid-1960s.

And then LeBron made good on his *other* promise and told the press the secret he'd teased a year earlier. The doubting words of people he worked with in Miami, he said, were what drove him to win. As he told ESPN:

"There were some people that I trusted and built relationships with in those four years who told me I was making the biggest mistake of my career [when I left the Heat]. And that right there was my motivation."

After winning a title in Cleveland in 2016 and taking the Cavs to two more NBA Finals, LeBron changed teams once more, this time heading to the storied Los Angeles Lakers for the 2018–19 NBA season. During that time, LeBron turned 35 years old, which is usually when professional basketball players start to slow down, score fewer points and rebounds, and begin to think about retirement. But LeBron wasn't willing to hang up his jersey just yet, so he dug deep and grew determined to defy the limits of age.

AGE IS JUST A NUMBER

In his youngest and oldest years playing ball, LeBron James proved that age doesn't really matter if you've got talent and drive. It usually takes time for a new player to learn the ropes once they join the NBA. Rookies often take a few seasons to develop and then start to peak. But LeBron always defied

STAT ⚡ **In the 10-year period from 2011 to 2020, teams led by LeBron James went to the NBA Finals nine times and won the championship four times.**

"BEFORE YOU CAN WIN THE GAME ON THE BASKETBALL COURT, YOU NEED TO WIN THE MENTAL AND EMOTIONAL GAME IN YOUR MIND."

expectations when it came to age. He performed surprisingly well in 2003–04, his first season in the NBA. Joining a select group of players in NBA history to debut at age 18, he averaged nearly 21 points and six assists per game, and was named the Rookie of the Year. In the 2004–05 season, 20-year-old LeBron averaged 27.2 points per game. His impressive stats raised the bar for rookie athletes. Almost two decades later, he would do the same for veteran athletes.

In the 2021–22 NBA season, 37-year-old LeBron averaged 30.3 points per game as a Laker and was named to a record 18th start in the NBA All-Star Game. He was once the youngest player with a triple-double (double digits in points, rebounds, and assists in the same game) at age 20, and is now the oldest player to score 30 points in a triple-double (just a few weeks before his 37th birthday).

STAP ⚡ LeBron James is the record holder for both youngest and oldest player to average more than 25 points a game in a season.

MAKE ROOM FOR NEW VENTURES

In addition to playing well, LeBron had the energy, stamina, and talent to make room for new endeavors in his life. In the summer before the start of the 2019–20 NBA season, he kept a full workout schedule while also filming his first starring role in a major movie, *Space Jam: A New Legacy*. He woke up every day at 3 a.m. so he could train and keep up his basketball skills before reporting to the set of *Space Jam*, where he'd shoot for 12 hours a day. His priority, though, hadn't changed since fourth grade. Sports came first:

"Even when I was shooting the movie, I knew what was most important. That was me getting ready for the fall. I always had that in the front of my mind. It's my personal pressure I'm putting on myself."

LIFE LESSONS FROM THE KING

- **TRUST YOUR INSTINCTS.**
- **FAMILY MATTERS MORE THAN ANYTHING.**
- **MONEY ISN'T ALWAYS THE MOST IMPORTANT THING.**
- **TURN CRITICISM INTO MOTIVATION AND PROVE THE NAYSAYERS WRONG.**
- **ALWAYS BE REACHING FOR THE NEXT LEVEL.**
- **YOU'RE NEVER TOO YOUNG OR TOO OLD TO FOLLOW YOUR DREAMS.**

LEARN FROM OTHERS AND LET OTHERS LEARN FROM YOU

There are a handful of special people who bolstered LeBron James' legendary NBA career and looked after his well-being. In addition to his mother, Gloria, that group consisted of his grandmother, his youth sports coaches, and his elite high school basketball coaches. Together they helped build his confidence and athletic skills so he could make it to the NBA by age 18. LeBron knows he was lucky to be in the care of people who had his best interests at heart, and who were there to help him navigate opportunities as they unfolded. When he looks back now, as a father, he is most grateful for the strength and support of his single mom and wonders how she did it on her own. He cites her as his "greatest influence."

"I had my mother to blanket me and to give me security. She was my mother, my father, my everything. She put me first. My mother taught me what devotion truly means. I have tried to pass along her example by helping kids who are growing up in single-parent homes."

With a strong family foundation to root him, he was able to grow as an athlete and seek out professional guidance when it was most needed.

SEEK OUT EXPERTS

When you're setting out to accomplish a goal, your best resource is other people who have already achieved it. It's the surest way to overcome obstacles or avoid common mistakes. LeBron wasn't too proud to look to those who came before him for wisdom. For example, before the 2011–12 NBA season, LeBron's Miami Heat didn't get a much-needed star center, but LeBron set out to learn some of the skills and techniques of the position by working out with one of the best centers of all time:

Hakeem Olajuwon. After hearing that Olajuwon had helped superstars Dwight Howard and Kobe Bryant expand their already excellent skill sets, he asked the Hall of Famer for help. He was looking to polish his low-post game.

Olajuwon was eager to help and happy to see LeBron working hard to learn. For three hours at a time over three days, LeBron put his ego aside to improve his game. Olajuwon took note:

"I like the way he carries himself," said Olajuwon. "Just his demeanor. He was very humble."

LeBron went on to utilize these new skills in the 2012 championship run, and he was more comfortable leaving the perimeter to work the low post.

"I saw all of the moves we worked on," Olajuwon would proudly say. "When you work with a player, the satisfaction is in knowing that now, when it counts, when it is valued, he is executing."

"SOMETIMES THE COACHES TELL ME TO BE SELFISH, BUT MY GAME WON'T LET ME BE SELFISH."

LEARN HOW TO WIN

When LeBron played for the Cleveland Cavaliers during the first seven years of his career, the team didn't have a winning mindset because it had never captured a championship. LeBron clashed with coaches and didn't always see eye to eye with his teammates on executing plays.

Just four years before his arrival, the Miami Heat won a title with Dwyane Wade, and he was still around to mentor LeBron. Erik Spoelstra had taken over as head coach after serving as a Heat assistant coach for over a decade under Pat Riley and Stan Van Gundy. Riley, who won four titles as head coach of the Los Angeles Lakers in the 1980s, became a Heat executive when Spoelstra was promoted. LeBron felt he could acquire a great deal of knowledge just by being around these mentors and by being an active participant in the program:

"Being a part of that culture allowed me to grow, allowed me to see what it takes to not only compete for a championship but also to win a championship."

LeBron wasn't content to wait for a championship to come to him. He took the initiative to go to Miami to learn how to win. His growth as a player had hit its limit in Cleveland, but the sky was the limit in Miami.

EVOLVE FROM MENTEE TO MENTOR

The skills he developed and the new perspective he gained from working with a new set of mentors during his four years in Miami shaped the rest of LeBron's career. With a bigger role as a playmaker, increased efficiency in rebounds and assists, and the demeanor of an on-court general, LeBron won two titles in Miami. He returned to Cleveland with the heart and mind of a champion in 2014.

During the 2015–16 season, LeBron led the Cleveland Cavaliers by example, demonstrating that hard work and persistence were the way to a title. With the regular season and playoffs combined, the Cavs played more than 100 games that season, and LeBron suited up for every single one of them.

"FOR US TO BE ABLE TO END THIS, END THIS DROUGHT, OUR FANS DESERVE IT. AND IT WAS FOR THEM."

In the decisive game 7, LeBron played all 48 minutes. Kevin Arnovitz of ESPN paints the clearest picture of the moment when LeBron clinched victory:

"Just after drawing a 3-point foul on Ezeli, James again hunted the mismatch—drawing poor Ezeli off a pick-and-roll. As he has done so often, James guided the action to his left hand, took three dribbles, wiggled a sidestep with his left leg, then launched a 3-pointer over Ezeli that vaulted the Cavaliers into the lead 89-87. . . . It was the fateful stroke that defied history for Cleveland. . . . It was the moment when anyone with a pulse on the way strange events upend history in sports said, 'This might happen.'"

A few minutes later, the final score was 93-89, and Cleveland had won. After the game, the team celebrated in the locker room by chanting "automatic work," the motto LeBron introduced as a motivating catchphrase earlier that year. It was inscribed on the team's championship rings as a reminder that working hard and doing so consistently was the road to winning it all.

That winning season marked a turning point in LeBron's career: He'd transformed from a young player, soaking up knowledge and experience, to a seasoned mentor and a solid, hands-on team leader. This experience stayed with him. It followed him to the Los Angeles

A GOAT AMONG GOATS

At the beginning of the 2021–22 campaign, the NBA marked its 75th season by naming its greatest-of-all-time team. LeBron James not only landed a spot on the list, but he had dominated long enough to play alongside six other players on that illustrious squad: Russell Westbrook, Dwyane Wade, Shaquille O'Neal, Anthony Davis, Carmelo Anthony, and Ray Allen.

Lakers several years later, where a new coach named Frank Vogel and a young star named Anthony Davis would give LeBron a new opportunity to lead.

THINK LIKE A TEAMMATE

Leaders share what they've learned and experienced with others, and as such, offer their unique perspective. LeBron excelled as a leader, using his individual strengths to lift others up and push them to be their best.

In a team sport like basketball, leadership means collaboration. Good leaders recognize the goodness and possibility in others. LeBron is known as a player who shares on-court opportunities with his teammates. If he doesn't have a great shot, he will willingly and eagerly rebound and pass to someone with a better one.

LeBron follows only Michael Jordan in the statistic of all-time "plus minus." This means that when he's on the court, his teams play exponentially better than they do when he's taking a rest, and better than most other teams in NBA history. This is because LeBron doesn't just score baskets; he sets up plays for his teammates and dishes out assists.

STAT ⚡ LeBron is one of only seven NBA players to rack up over 10,000 assists.

"LEADERSHIP IS
NOT A
SOMETIMES THING.
IT'S AN
EVERYDAY THING."

"I HAVE NO PROBLEM BEING A ROLE MODEL. I LOVE IT."

It means a lot to LeBron that his legacy includes that aspect of his game. He told *USA Today* that he wants to be known as "one of the most unselfish players that played this game."

RAISE THE BAR

An NBA team needs everyone to be great, from the front office down to the towel boys. The same applies to just about any business or workplace. You can scale up your goals and reach bigger ones if you've got a group working toward the same result.

In 2014, when LeBron returned to Cleveland after two championships in four years with Miami, he arrived with the burden of teaching a roster of many young, inexperienced players how to win. LeBron described that experience as more challenging than trying to win his first championship. He started with what had worked in Miami, using what he saw Pat Riley and Erik Spoelstra do there, and applied that approach to the Cleveland Cavaliers. LeBron was instrumental in teaching the Cavs the three-star style of play. Having benefited from the super trio he'd formed with Dwyane Wade and Chris Bosh, LeBron formed a new one in Cleveland with Kevin Love and Kyrie Irving, two men who had never made a deep playoff run but had the talent, drive, and focus to join up with LeBron.

During this second era in Cleveland, LeBron organized players-only meetings and workouts, texting his teammates directly to ensure they'd attend and to hold them accountable.

LeBron acted, as much as he could, like a coach. His boldness and the combined work of his teammates culminated in triumph. Two years after his return to Ohio, the Cavaliers won the NBA title.

LIFE LESSONS FROM THE KING

- OBSERVE AND LEARN FROM EXPERTS IN YOUR FIELD.

- SHARE THE LESSONS YOU LEARNED SO YOU CAN BE A LEADER AND MENTOR OTHERS.

- SHOW STRENGTH, BUT BALANCE IT WITH HUMILITY AND COOPERATION.

- SET A HIGH LEVEL OF EXPECTATION FOR YOURSELF, AND ENCOURAGE OTHERS TO RISE TO IT.

"I THINK 'TEAM FIRST.' IT ALLOWS ME TO SUCCEED, AND IT ALLOWS MY TEAMS TO SUCCEED."

WAIT FOR YOUR MOMENT

There's a lot more to achievement than physical toil, hard work, and pushing to be better. Successful people, particularly elite athletes like LeBron James, know that winning anything requires getting into the proper headspace and, sometimes, waiting for things to click. That can be just as grueling and require as much commitment as getting your body in shape. But all that patience, strategizing, and visualizing can pay off handsomely. It makes the will to succeed stronger, and a strong will yields maximum results.

PATIENCE BALANCES PASSION

Truly successful people stay committed, and a hefty dose of patience sustains the determination to reach a goal over the course of many years. LeBron committed himself to winning a title in high school, and he kept that at the forefront of his mind every time he practiced and played with the rest of the "Fabulous Four" at St. Vincent–St. Mary in Akron, Ohio, in the late 1990s.

He took the long view as a professional, too, enduring many arduous seasons with the Cleveland Cavaliers as they worked to slowly improve, soldiering on through the scrutiny and pressure of his first season with the Heat on the long road to capturing that coveted NBA title:

"The Greater Man upstairs know when it's my time. Right now isn't the time."

LeBron has always demonstrated a tireless commitment to basketball, working every angle so he can set his teams up for success, whether it's practicing hard or recruiting players. Then he waits for the work to pay off.

BUILD TOWARD YOUR DREAMS

Winning an NBA championship is a dream and a goal for any professional player. It was no different for LeBron. Even though he was heralded as "The Chosen One" as far back as 2002, when he was still in high school and more

"I KNOW I'M THE BEST HIGH SCHOOL PLAYER IN THE WORLD, BUT ONCE YOU GET DRAFTED, IT'S TIME TO START BACK OVER."

"MY GRANDMOTHER TAUGHT ME BEFORE SHE PASSED AWAY, 'THE GOOD THINGS COME TO THE GUYS WHO ARE PATIENT AND THANKFUL FOR WHAT THEY HAVE IN FRONT OF THEM.'"

"I'M CHASING WHAT I CAN POTENTIALLY DO."

than a year away from being the first pick in the 2003 NBA draft, he would have to wait a long time to get a championship ring. But he watched as, little by little, he inched closer to his goal. In 2002–03, the Cavs won 17 games. The following season, their first with LeBron, they won 35. The next year they had a winning record of 42–40 but missed the playoffs for the second year in a row. While it was a particularly competitive Eastern Conference that year, it was the seventh straight year of the Cavs missing the playoffs. There was still a lot more work left to do.

In 2006, the Cavs improved again, to 50-32, but they ended up losing in the second round of the playoffs. Finally, after four

---

STAT ⚡ In his second season, LeBron James made the Cavaliers into viable contenders, giving them their first winning record in seven years, leading the league in minutes played and ranking third in scoring (with 27.2 PPG), third in steals, and sixth in assists. That season, he also became the youngest player in NBA history to score a 50-point game.

LEAVE IT ALL ON THE FLOOR

LeBron was so depleted after his explosive game 5 performance in the Eastern Conference finals in 2007 that he was given an IV in the locker room.

years of hard-earned progress, the 2007 Cavaliers looked better than ever. They fought their way to the Eastern Conference finals and in a pivotal game 5 of that series, LeBron blew up to score 29 of Cleveland's last 30 points against the Detroit Pistons, including the game-winning layup with two seconds left in double overtime, finishing with 48 points, nine rebounds, and seven assists. The Cavs went on to win game 6 and advanced to the NBA Finals for the first time in franchise history.

Unfortunately, they didn't have long to enjoy their victory. They were swept in the NBA Finals by the San Antonio Spurs. LeBron didn't know it then, but it wouldn't be his last chance to compete at that level. Two seasons later, the Cavs won their division with 66 wins, a franchise record. They won 61 games the following season. That's about the time when LeBron decided that patience had run its course and decisive action was needed. He followed his gut and left Cleveland in 2010 to play for Miami.

"I THINK EVERY SEASON FOR ME IS ALL ABOUT PATIENCE."

KEEP YOUR EYE ON THE PRIZE

Still, LeBron would have to wait even longer to hoist the Larry O'Brien Championship Trophy, parlaying his patience and anxiousness into serious work, and focusing on his game and that of his teammates, carefully biding his time as he built himself into championship material.

In 2011, at the end of his first season with the Miami Heat, LeBron reached the NBA Finals once again, but the Heat eventually lost to the Dallas Mavericks. LeBron was disappointed with himself, again having almost reached the top and falling short. Managing frustration was always one of the hardest parts of his job:

"Sometimes in the past when I played, something might make me lose focus, or I would go home after a game where I thought I could have played better and I would let it hang over my head for a long time when it shouldn't."

Rather than letting frustration take over, LeBron went back to work, analyzing what elements of his game he needed to improve and how he could be more effective in high-pressure situations.

After another year of intense effort and as much patience as he could muster, LeBron led the Miami Heat to victory in the NBA Finals. At that point, reaching the last stage of the NBA playoffs had become routine for LeBron. He'd

---

STAT ⚡ **LeBron James is the only NBA player to rank in the Top 100 in points, assists, rebounds, steals, blocks, *and* 3-pointers. As of 2021, he ranked No. 3 in points, No. 8 in assists, No. 42 in rebounds, No. 11 in steals, No. 100 in blocks, and No. 11 in 3-pointers made.**

---

hit the NBA Finals four years in a row with the Heat (winning once more), and then make another four consecutive trips during his second tenure in Cleveland (where he'd win again). And with the storied and prestigious Los Angeles Lakers, LeBron would reach the NBA Finals by the time his second season rolled around.

FAILURE IS PART OF THE PROCESS

Failure is a part of life, and it's also a part of the game. Not even King James can win *every* game he plays or take his team to the NBA Finals every year. LeBron-led teams won the NBA Finals four times, but they also lost the finals six times. LeBron has missed clutch, potentially game-winning shots. Over the course of his career, he's whiffed about a quarter of his easy-to-make free throw attempts and missed a third of all shot attempts. For every three games he's played, he's lost one. And yet, in terms of NBA basketball stats, that qualifies as exceptional because losing is built into the game. Perfection has never been the goal for LeBron James; improvement and overall achievement are his purpose:

"When I have a bad game, it continues to humble me and know that, you know, you still have work to do and you still have lots of people to impress."

LeBron faces losses like every other professional basketball player. But it's what he does in response to those errors and losses that sets him apart and makes him a champion. With grit and determination, he's able to brush off the mistakes, take an honest look at himself and his performance, and improve on it as much as he can.

In the 2011 NBA Finals, he was widely criticized for not playing hard enough. But he wasn't interested in judging himself by everyone else's standards: It was when his performance didn't meet his own standard that he struggled the most. Losing the NBA Finals that year was one of the lowest moments in LeBron's career, but he now reflects on it as one of the best things that's ever happened to him. It changed his outlook:

"It took me to go all the way to the top and then hit rock bottom to realize what I needed to do as a professional athlete and a person. I played to prove people wrong instead of just playing my game, instead of just going out and having fun and playing a game that I grew up loving."

FOLLOW YOUR FORTUNE

In his business ventures, LeBron James knows the value of waiting for the right moment and investing in his own ideas. In 2012, LeBron's national endorsement contract with McDonald's expired. Rather than re-sign to the tune of a small fortune, LeBron (along with business partner Maverick Carter and financial adviser Paul Wachter) put his fast-food interests elsewhere. LeBron invested under $1 million in Blaze Pizza, a California-based start-up restaurant chain. Five years later, that relatively small investment paid off handsomely. Blaze expanded so quickly and to such success that the stake in the company left LeBron and his associates $25 million richer. With

newfound trust in the company and in his own instincts, LeBron agreed to be the company's spokesman.

TURN LEMONS INTO LEMONADE

Sometimes losing is a combination of your own shortcomings and things beyond your control. We all get dealt a bad hand at some point. LeBron and the Miami Heat failed to win the 2014 NBA Finals, having been outmatched by a superior, star-studded San Antonio Spurs squad. The Heat's huge loss in the first game in the series (by 15 points) came in part because they lost LeBron for the crucial fourth quarter—the lack of air-conditioning in the Spurs' arena (in Texas in June) led to extreme physical discomfort for players on both sides. It got so bad for LeBron that the ensuing dehydration and cramps forced him to exit the game, allowing the Spurs to run up the score:

"I lost all the fluids that I was putting in in the last couple of days out there on the floor. It sucks not being out there for your team, especially at this point in the season."

"ALL YOU CONTINUE
TO DO IS KEEP
THE FOCUS OUT
ON THE FLOOR . . .
AND NOT FALL INTO A
LOSING MENTALITY."

> ## "SITTING ON THE SIDELINE, YOU KNOW, IF I'M NOT IN FOUL TROUBLE, IS NOT GOOD FOR US AND NOT GOOD FOR ME."

LeBron reflected on those game-ending, game-losing cramps for years. There wasn't anything he could do to erase the past, but he did manage to find a way to leverage that career setback into a new business venture. Four years later, in 2018, LeBron used that low moment to inspire Ladder, a nutritional supplements company he started with Arnold Schwarzenegger that specializes in products for high-performance athletes, including supplements designed to prevent muscle cramps in the heat of competition. The company remains profitable today with over 130,000 subscribers and millions in sales revenue.

SECOND CHANCES DO COME ALONG

In 2004, at age 19 and with a single NBA season under his belt, LeBron James was selected for the roster of the USA Men's Basketball team. The national squad competed in the Summer Olympics in Athens that year, and along with LeBron included major basketball stars of the era, such as former Most Valuable Players Allen Iverson and Tim Duncan as well as Carmelo Anthony and Dwyane Wade. This fourth iteration of the "Dream Team," so named because the Olympics allowed the U.S. to field a team consisting of professionals, was so stacked that LeBron, the reigning NBA Rookie of the Year, saw very little playing time. While he hit the court in all eight of the team's games, he didn't get a chance to make a mark. He turned out the most underwhelming stats of his career (high school and the NBA), averaging 5.4 points, 1.6 assists, and one rebound per game. It was only the third time that the Americans didn't bring home the gold. Instead of dwelling on the disappointment of not being asked to contribute or the fact that Team USA went home with the bronze medal, LeBron focused on the next opportunity and stayed positive.

He waited for his second chance: the 2008 Olympics. He was once again invited to play for Team USA, but this time, the coaches put him to good use. With 15.7 points and 2.3 steals per game, he led the American team in those categories and helped them win the gold medal. LeBron's performance, a vast improvement on his work from four years earlier, helped earn the team the nickname "The Redeem Team."

LET GO OF YOUR GRUDGES

A legend like LeBron knows that holding a grudge offers no value. If you allow them to, grudges will throw you off your game, taint your point of view, and cause you to lose focus. They don't fuel passion, creativity, or hard work. They just distract you from the goal at hand.

When the Heat came to town to play the Cavaliers after LeBron moved to Miami, hundreds of people who had once cheered him on were suddenly booing him. Fans who felt betrayed by his departure were eager to let him know how they felt.

"IT WAS A DREAM COME TRUE FOR ME TO REPRESENT MY COUNTRY."

"NEGATIVITY, BAD ENERGY, HATE, ENVY . . . WILL TRY TO BRING YOU DOWN THROUGHOUT YOUR JOURNEY, AND IT'S UP TO YOU ON HOW YOU HANDLE IT."

"YOUR HATE MAKES ME STRONGER."

How did LeBron respond? He didn't. He resisted the temptation to engage with the negativity. He played through. He put his focus on achieving the goal that sent him to Miami in the first place and, in the end, delivered two NBA titles to his fans in Miami. Because he didn't carry any harsh feelings toward Cleveland—on the contrary, his charities helped support and improve life in impoverished areas of northeastern Ohio—he felt pretty good about returning to the Cavaliers in 2014. He allowed bygones to be bygones and even sought out team owner Gilbert in an effort to smooth things over:

"I've met with Dan, face-to-face, man-to-man. We've talked it out. Everybody makes mistakes. I've made mistakes as well. Who am I to hold a grudge?"

LeBron approached his return to Cleveland with sensibility, respect, and maturity. They found a way forward with the shared goal of winning a championship for Cleveland.

DEVELOP AN ATTITUDE OF GRATITUDE

In his chosen role as a mentor and team leader, gratitude is a quality that LeBron makes sure to pass on to those who look up to him for life lessons and guidance. Once he made the move back to Cleveland, he knew he had to instill a culture that was conducive to winning:

"I've taken on the burden of leading young guys. Getting them to understand what it takes to win. And it takes more than just basketball. It's about being a professional, not having a sense of entitlement, being grateful that you're a part of this league."

"I'M A BLESSED KID."

He knows that when players let their egos be their guide, it becomes difficult to work and win as a team. With a shared appreciation and a little camaraderie, the Cavs could unify around a common goal. Gratitude was also useful in deflecting the negative feedback that sometimes flowed in from the public and the press. LeBron tried to model a healthy attitude that kept it all in perspective. When asked about widespread ridicule of his latest social media posts, LeBron responded, "I've got a beautiful family, beautiful teammates, and this game of basketball has brought me so much, so the outside noises just really don't affect me."

With no personal vendetta to get in the way of more important things, it was that much easier for LeBron to get down to the business of basketball, and in 2016, his Cavaliers won the NBA Finals, the first championship in team history.

MAKE A BOLD PLAN AND FOLLOW IT

After re-signing Dwyane Wade, the Heat picked up Chris Bosh and LeBron and completed the power trio that would be called "The Big Three." As soon as LeBron got to Miami, he was already envisioning huge success. He declared that Miami would win "not two, not three, not four, not five, not six, not seven" championships, but more. They lost the 2011 NBA Finals. But they did go on to complete step one of LeBron's bold declarations in 2012.

After winning his first NBA title, LeBron was instantly dreaming even bigger: "I know I can get better," he said. "And I know I'm not satisfied with one of these."

"YOU DON'T GET A PASS FOR NOT PRACTICING EXCELLENCE EVERY DAY, AND TRYING TO BE GREAT EVERY DAY."

FINALS STREAKS

LeBron went to four straight NBA Finals with the Miami Heat from 2011 to 2014 (and won two). He went to four straight Finals again with Cleveland from 2015 to 2018 (and won one). He has made 10 NBA Finals appearances over the course of his career, winning four and losing six.

Since winning the 2012 NBA Finals, LeBron has been back to the championship round over and over again. He's captured four NBA titles, bringing victory to every franchise he's played for: the Cleveland Cavaliers, the Miami Heat, and the Los Angeles Lakers. At age 37, he was the oldest player in NBA history to contend for an annual scoring title. He owns sports teams, he gives back to his hometown in a meaningful and lasting way, and he has an estimated net worth of $850 million. LeBron dreamed hard, and then worked even harder toward making all those wildly difficult-to-achieve aspirations a part of his reality.

Even with all of these achievements, LeBron can't help but set his sights even higher. Throughout LeBron's career, no matter how much he accomplished, he often felt as though he was standing in the shadow of the

"I'M VERY COMFORTABLE BEING UNCOMFORTABLE."

great Michael Jordan. The debate as to who was a superior player loomed large, with many people citing Jordan's six championship rings as the deciding factor. LeBron admitted to *Sports Illustrated* in 2016 that he was "chasing the ghost" of Michael Jordan:

"I looked up to him so much. I think it's cool to put myself in position to be one of those great players, but if I can ever put myself in position to be the greatest player, that would be something extraordinary."

LIFE LESSONS FROM THE KING

- SUCCESS TAKES TIME.

- MISTAKES AND FAILURE ARE INEVITABLE IN ANY PURSUIT.

- CARRYING GRUDGES DOESN'T MOTIVATE YOU; IT DRAINS YOU.

- BEING THANKFUL GIVES YOUR WORK MEANING AND MOTIVATES YOU MORE.

- TAKE SMALL STEPS TOWARD YOUR BIGGEST DREAMS.

TRY NEW THINGS

LeBron James is more than just a stellar basketball player. He's a businessman, an actor, an activist, an entrepreneur, and a man who wears many hats in public. That's because opportunities abound, and LeBron has never been shy about grabbing them when they come his way, nor does he hesitate to pursue projects that he's excited about or that benefit himself, his family, his community, or the NBA. Even when it comes to his position on the court, LeBron understands the potential payoff of trying something new.

He's played basketball at the professional and Olympic level, but he has also pursued comedic acting, worked on animated films, formed charities, helped create a media mouthpiece for athletes called Uninterrupted, started a production company, and invested in a number of businesses to satisfy his endless hunger for success and curiosity about how far his reach can go.

FIND WHAT YOU DO BEST

When LeBron entered the NBA with the Cleveland Cavaliers in 2003, he primarily played small forward because his team already had a veteran power forward in Carlos Boozer. Small forwards are physically smaller than power forwards, take more outside and midrange shots, and handle the ball more, leaving the more hulking power forwards to muscle their way in for layups and inside shots while also handling defense.

Early in his first season with the Miami Heat in 2011–12, coach Erik Spoelstra tried LeBron in the markedly different position of point guard. He'd been a point guard in high school and understood that it meant being the general of the team on offense. He gave it his best, taking the ball from one end of the court to the other and setting up and facilitating plays for the rest of his squad. But after two months in that position, despite his earlier experience, the Heat determined that LeBron was a more effective scorer when someone else fed him the ball.

As the season progressed, LeBron moved to power forward, having already put many pounds of muscle on his once-lean frame and having also developed his inside and low-post game skills. This was where the Heat needed him most since power forwards Chris Bosh and Udonis Haslem were out with injuries. LeBron's defensive skills were so strong that he averaged more points and rebounds per game and was named to the NBA's All-Defensive First Team.

STAT ⚡ Only five players in NBA history have ever amassed more than 100 triple-doubles, games in which they achieve double digits in three out of five individual statistical categories: points, rebounds, assists, steals, and blocks. LeBron achieved his 100th triple-double in December 2021.

"IF YOU TAKE
A SHORTCUT
OR IF YOU DON'T
HANDLE BUSINESS,
THEN YOU
COME UP SHORT."

"I'M CONFIDENT WITH MY ABILITY."

Finding his place as a power forward seemed to be the final piece of the puzzle for LeBron. That year marked the first time his team would win an NBA title, with the Miami Heat defeating the Oklahoma City Thunder 4-1. The following season, with LeBron fully entrenched as the team's primary power forward, the Heat won another NBA championship.

BE FLEXIBLE

The versatility that LeBron showed in adapting to various positions on the court helped to cement his legendary status. When LeBron returned to the Cleveland Cavaliers, his coaches asked him to adapt yet again, returning to the small forward position. He wasn't thrilled about the change, but he brought a whole new skill set and perspective to that position in his 2015–16 season with the Cavs. It was one of the key factors that led to them winning the NBA championship in June 2016.

Having found his niche, you'd think LeBron would be content to stay at power forward *or* small forward. But years later, he was ready to prove that he could be all things on the court if needed. In December 2021, his Los Angeles Lakers lost five games in a row. Assistant coach David Fizdale pinpointed one of the sources of the problem as the center position. Starting center DeAndre Jordan just wasn't working out, so Fizdale decided to put LeBron in that spot.

With LeBron acting as the big man in the middle, the Lakers beat the Houston Rockets, bolstered by his 32 points and 11 assists.

LeBron wasn't overstating when he said, "I'm always trying to keep myself in a position where I could be anywhere on the floor." Over the course of his NBA career and during his time on the USA Men's Basketball Team at the Olympics, LeBron played all five positions: shooting guard, point guard, center, power forward, and small forward. He has the skills required for every position, and he uses them to make his team stronger:

"I've taken pride over my career in being able to play five positions or at least know all five positions. If I'm guarding a big, what is the coverage? If I'm guarding a small, what's the coverage?"

LeBron does what it takes to win, and in handling all positions so expertly, he made versatility a key quality to value in a player.

EMBRACE YOUR CREATIVE SIDE

Following Bill Russell (1979), Michael Jordan (1991), and Charles Barkley (1993), in September 2007, LeBron James became only the

"PRESSURE IS BUILT WHEN YOU'RE SUCCESSFUL AT ONLY ONE THING."

fourth professional basketball player to host *Saturday Night Live*. The late-night sketch comedy show is usually guest hosted by an actor, comedian, or another entertainer, but LeBron, as famous as any movie star or pop musician, got the gig of hosting the 33rd season opener despite zero acting experience (outside of TV commercials and cameos where he played himself).

He had such a positive experience venturing outside of his comfort zone that he embraced more opportunities to act, specifically in comedy projects. In 2015, he starred as a fictionalized version of himself in the Amy Schumer comedy *Trainwreck*, playing a client of a world-renowned physical therapist played by *SNL* star Bill Hader.

DON'T BE AFRAID TO ASK

When *Trainwreck* director and co-writer Judd Apatow asked LeBron to make a brief cameo in the movie, LeBron saw an even bigger opportunity. He and business partner Maverick Carter asked for a more significant role, the role of Hader's best friend. Apatow agreed. LeBron received heaps of praise from movie critics for his performance. *The New York Times* said he was "a surprisingly limber comic presence," while Slate called him "the best part of this movie."

In 2018, he tried another new thing: animation. He portrayed the bigfoot-like character Gwangi in the hit animated comedy *Smallfoot*. Then in 2021, he played both the live-action and animated version

"I'M LIKE A SUPERHERO. CALL ME BASKETBALL MAN."

of himself in the mixed-media basketball sci-fi adventure *Space Jam: A New Legacy*, a follow-up to the 1996 film starring Michael Jordan. He grew up watching Looney Tunes and looked up to Jordan, so the project meant a lot to him. He also liked the message that the movie offered to kids:

> *"I'd just love for kids to understand how empowered they can feel and how empowered they can be if they don't just give up on their dreams."*

Acting was something LeBron had been interested in for a long time, so he grabbed these unique opportunities and created new experiences for himself:

> *"I always talked about it as a kid, and even as an adult. I was like, 'Wow, you know, I always wanted to be the Fresh Prince of Bel-Air.' And then when I got older, I was like, 'I would love to do an action movie,' Either be, like a cop or something, or be, like Batman."*

Never afraid to venture out beyond his comfort zone or to usurp a larger role in a game or a movie, LeBron made bold moves in acting and entertainment that helped build his legacy as a cultural icon.

GET DOWN TO BUSINESS

LeBron James always wanted to be a great athlete or the greatest basketball player of all time. He accomplished that, and he continues to add as many pursuits as his fame and free time afford him. Becoming an entertainer and telling Black stories is now a top priority in his life. It's one of the reasons why he moved to Los Angeles, uprooting himself from his second stint playing near his hometown in Cleveland. He wanted to be closer to the entertainment industry, lay down roots in the entertainment capital of the United States, and look toward his post-basketball future as an entertainer, businessman, and mogul.

In 2020, LeBron and Maverick Carter formed SpringHill Company by merging three other companies they created: entertainment production company SpringHill Entertainment, formed in 2007; marketing and branding agency The Robot Company; and Uninterrupted, an athlete's platform for nonathletic projects. They signed a scripted deal with ABC Signature in 2020, and then a four-year deal with Universal Pictures. "LeBron and I have always been interested in the long game," said Carter. "And the long game here is to build a media company."

SpringHill is named after the modest apartment complex in Akron where LeBron lived with his mother from age 12 to 18. The name reminds LeBron of his humble roots and the importance of telling compelling stories about human beings from all neighborhoods. Among the films in which LeBron had a hand are *What's My Name: Muhammad Ali,* a documentary for HBO; *Dreamland: The Burning of Black Wall Street* for HBO; *Hustle,* a basketball movie he made with Adam Sandler; *Self-Made,* a Netflix biography about Black businesswoman C. J. Walker; *The Wall*, a philanthropic game show; the Starz drama *Survivor's Remorse*; and the talk show *The Shop*, which LeBron hosts himself from a barbershop, a cornerstone of many Black communities.

"I MAKE IMPACT PLAYS. I MAKE GAME-CHANGING PLAYS."

When Warner Bros. wanted LeBron to star in *Space Jam: A New Legacy*, he and Carter agreed but asked for more than a salary. LeBron wanted a production deal to make more movies, TV shows, and online content. Warner Bros. agreed and quickly invested $15.8 million in Uninterrupted, bringing it under the banner of NBA game broadcaster Turner Sports. It is important to LeBron to build his business his way:

"We're still climbing Mount Kilimanjaro, but having this group of people, who can put together my thoughts and bring them to fruition, is the vision that I had 10-plus years ago."

SEEK OUT NEW PARTNERSHIPS

Even in the early years of his fame, LeBron dared to venture beyond the business of basketball into other sports and industries. His leadership roles expanded in ways that no one expected, and his influence grew. In 2011, LeBron signed with branding and marketing company Fenway Sports Group. His image and endorsements were already so valuable that FSG, a new and unproven company, paid him with a stake in Liverpool FC, one of the most popular and famous soccer teams in England's Premier League. Just two years later, LeBron had surpassed Kobe Bryant as the world's richest basketball player. Ten years after joining as a client, LeBron became a partner and co-owner, giving him lucrative stakes in the Boston Red Sox and a larger share of Liverpool FC.

LeBron also delved into music in 2018 and 2019, serving as executive producer on major rapper 2 Chainz's 2019 album, *Rap or Go to the League*. According to a press release, the album was about "celebrating Black excellence" and "the power of education and entrepreneurship," two concepts close to LeBron's heart. The title reflects a proverb about inner-city life for many young Black men, that the only way out of their tough neighborhoods is through music or sports. LeBron wanted to make art that gave voice to that experience:

TRADEMARK TOSS

Part of LeBron James' bevy of pre-game activities involves throwing a handful of talcum powder into the air. Nicknamed the "chalk toss," LeBron started the tradition in 2003 to keep his hands dry for the start of the game. Fans cheered on the spectacle of it, so he kept doing it, both as a bit of showmanship for the crowd and as a grounding pre-game ritual for himself.

"I'm doing this piece with 2 Chainz. I'm doing a TV series with Octavia Spencer. I'm doing Space Jam *with Ryan Coogler. So for me to be able to push all this, and let these kids know that we have so much to tell— so many great stories. . . . For me, being in this position means a lot."*

REMEMBER TO HAVE FUN

LeBron has always embraced his fun side, no matter what he's doing. For example, in January 2013, a man named Michael Drysch had the chance to win $150,000 if he made a half-court shot during halftime at a Miami Heat game. If he hooked it in, he'd win $75,000 for himself and $75,000 for the

"I'M ALL ABOUT PUSHING THE AFRICAN AMERICAN CULTURE."

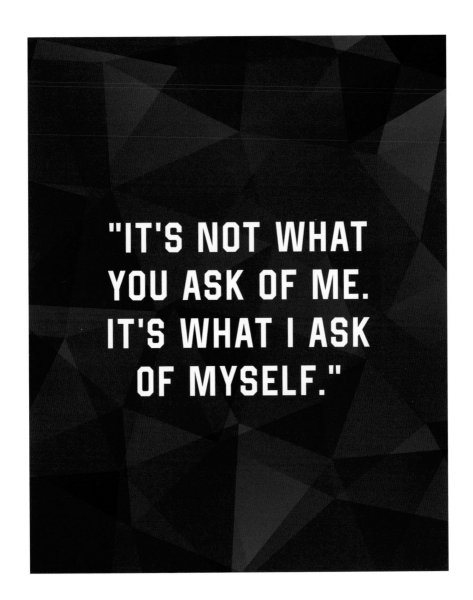

"IT'S NOT WHAT YOU ASK OF ME. IT'S WHAT I ASK OF MYSELF."

Boys and Girls Clubs of America via The LeBron James Family Foundation. Amazingly, Drysch made the near-impossible shot. As he celebrated, Drysch was tackled to the floor by a laughing, screaming, celebrating LeBron, who watched the whole thing unfold and ran over from the team bench to congratulate the lucky guy.

KEEP AN OPEN MIND

LeBron James never limited himself to just one path to success. During the 2011–12 season, NBA players and team owners couldn't reach a collective bargaining agreement. While he waited for the agreeable resolution (which ultimately came) and waited out the downtime that he would otherwise

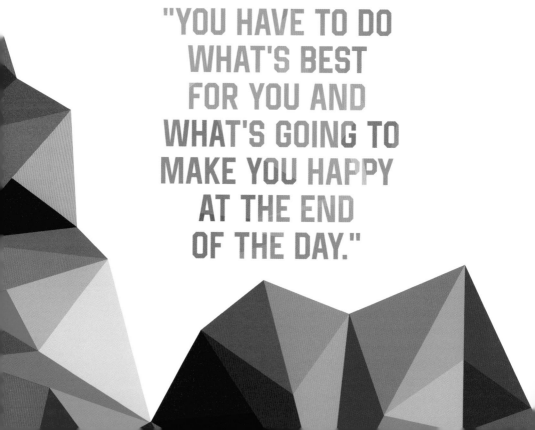

"YOU HAVE TO DO WHAT'S BEST FOR YOU AND WHAT'S GOING TO MAKE YOU HAPPY AT THE END OF THE DAY."

have spent playing basketball, LeBron considered the possibility of walking away from the game altogether. A two-sport star in high school, he'd been an excellent wide receiver, and at age 27, he seriously considered giving the NFL a shot. Dallas Cowboys owner Jerry Jones even offered LeBron a spot on the team, and the Seattle Seahawks invited him to work out with their players. "I would have made the team," LeBron later boasted. "I would have tried out, but I would have made the team."

LIFE LESSONS FROM THE KING

- **BE VERSATILE AND EXPAND YOUR VALUE.**
- **EXPLORE YOUR DEEPEST INTERESTS.**
- **ASK FOR WHAT YOU REALLY WANT.**
- **HAVE FUN NO MATTER WHAT YOU DO.**

"WHO I AM AS A MAN AND WHAT I DO OFF THE FLOOR DEFINES MY LEGACY MORE THAN WHAT I DO ON THE FLOOR."

GET WITH YOUR GROUP

Basketball requires you to count on your team. It's difficult, if not impossible, to reach the top all alone. For a sports legend like LeBron James, it sometimes looks from the outside as though his on-court accomplishments represent the efforts of one man. But he wouldn't be able to take the court and impress fans with that many points, rebounds, and assists if he didn't have a solid team behind him.

LeBron started life with a tight-knit family unit. He was raised by his mother, Gloria, in his grandmother's house, with the assistance of uncles and friends of the family. That love and support provided emotional stability for LeBron, a safe place that served as a launching point for his achievements. It also marked the start of a career-long habit of his, surrounding himself with dependable, time-tested people with his best interests in mind. Whether they're a biological family or a chosen family made up of friends, advisers, and teammates, LeBron ensures that he builds a trustworthy group to rely on without fail, and he provides the same for them.

WORK WELL WITH OTHERS

As a fifth grader on the Northeast Shooting Stars, an Akron, Ohio–based team in the Amateur Athletic Union, LeBron at first focused entirely on getting buckets, taking every shot himself and assuming the role as the team's leading scorer. That approach changed when Coach Dru Joyce II taught LeBron that there were always four other teammates on the court at any given time, and that they all wanted to win, and they all had skills. That simple lesson—to learn to see past yourself to who is open, and then set them up for a good shot—transformed LeBron's game. Not only did his teammates' scoring rates go up, but LeBron started racking up assists, a step on the road to becoming a more well-rounded player. "That was the last

time that I ever had to talk about LeBron shooting too much. He just got it," Joyce said.

That camaraderie on the court extended to their personal lives. The Northeast Shooting Stars were more than an AAU team to LeBron. They were a family, a band of brothers in basketball battle. "The Fab Five," as they called themselves, stuck together as a competitive unit for years. LeBron, Sian Cotton, Romeo Travis, Willie McGee, and Dru Joyce III even made the decision to all attend the same high school together, St. Vincent–St. Mary in Akron, so they could be in the same basketball program under a promising, innovative coach. Those five players knew each other's game so deeply that playing together had become second nature. The strong bond and friendship led to three Ohio state basketball titles and a connection that would last for years.

FIND PARTNERS YOU TRUST

The Fab Five helped to insulate LeBron with a buffer zone of tried-and-true friends in his early playing years. But the friendship that would have the most lasting impact on his career was the one he struck up with Maverick Carter when Carter was a star senior on St. Vincent–St. Mary's basketball team and LeBron was a freshman. He eventually became the chief architect of LeBron's business and entrepreneurial career and LeBron's trusted friend and adviser. Carter is one of a group of lifelong friends of LeBron who have, at various points, helped bolster his success, kept him grounded, and made their own mark.

Though LeBron was about 20 years old and relatively new to the NBA and the business side of basketball, he already wanted to have more control over his future and success. In 2005, two years into his NBA career, LeBron parted ways with his longtime agents, Aaron and Eric Goodwin, to form LRMR, a marketing and sports agency, with Carter, Rich Paul, and Randy Mims, all people LeBron had known since childhood. He knew he needed strong, trustworthy advisers, so LeBron recruited his most business-minded friends, particularly Carter and Paul, and eschewed conventional wisdom to hire more seasoned advisers. LeBron refers to his inner circle as "The Four Horsemen":

> *"I knew I had to grow as a businessperson. So why not let the guys around me grow with me?"*

When asked to reflect on whether he was ready for the pitfalls of fame and money when he entered the NBA, LeBron responded, "I was ready because I had my friends. They were my shelter; they made me stay humble." The value of The Four Horsemen went far beyond their business advice. They weren't just "yes men" who would indulge LeBron's ego:

> *"[My friends] had no stars in their eyes about me like so many others did. Their attitude was, 'You're still LeBron James. Don't put on any airs with us; we know who you are.' They never glorified me."*

"I STAY HUMBLE BECAUSE TOMORROW ISN'T PROMISED, AND YOU NEVER KNOW WHAT MAY HAPPEN."

TELLING HIS STORY

One of LeBron's first entertainment ventures was the 2009 film *More Than a Game*. The documentary is LeBron's life story, tracking his unlikely and bold ascent (along with his close-knit group of teammates) to the top of Ohio high school basketball and the local AAU circuit.

LISTEN TO THE EXPERTS

LeBron also hired investor Paul Wachter to help him and his associates properly invest LeBron's growing finances and pursue solid business interests. LeBron has always had a keen interest in high-performance bicycles, so in 2007, Wachter suggested that LRMR buy a large stake in Cannondale Bicycle Corporation. The company quadrupled in value within a year, and LeBron and his associates sold their shares and made tens of millions. The next year, acting on Wachter's recommendation, LeBron acquired a small stake in the headphone company Beats Electronics. He agreed to be the company's spokesperson and be paid to wear Beats headphones in public in exchange for a piece of the company instead of a flat endorsement fee.

When Beats Electronics was sold to Apple Computer for more than $1 billion in 2014, LeBron's deferred and denied payment wound up netting him $30 million. On the heels of that deal, in 2015, Wachter negotiated one of the biggest athlete shoe deals in history. LeBron signed a pioneering lifelong contract with industry leader Nike. The branding and endorsement of high-end athletic equipment in LeBron's name will reportedly pay out as much as $1 billion over time.

ASK FOR HELP

During LeBron's first era with the Cleveland Cavaliers, he frequently lobbied the team's front office to bring in players of a higher caliber, ones who shared not only his deep desire and focus to win championships but who were also

on a similar All-Star level. Neither he, nor the Cavaliers' executives, could persuade any players of note to join the LeBron "family" in the mid-2000s: "A lot of people didn't want to come to Cleveland. I tried to recruit so many guys to come to Cleveland... and it just didn't work out."

Among those stars who resisted LeBron's offers: Joe Johnson, Michael Redd, and Chris Bosh. However, when LeBron flipped from the Cavaliers to the Miami Heat in 2010, Heat executives quickly got on board and heard LeBron's argument that they needed to recruit more stars if they wanted to win championships. With LeBron, Bosh, and Wade already on the roster, standouts like Shane Battier and Ray Allen were easier to recruit. During LeBron's four seasons in Miami, the Heat made it to the NBA Finals every year, and they won twice. LeBron's team of strong, carefully chosen players, a close-knit team he had a hand in building, made that possible.

One of the biggest lessons LeBron learned in Miami: Even an unparalleled superstar can't win a championship by himself. He needed other superstars who understood and carried out his style of play. The Cavaliers learned this, too—the hard way. In those four years when LeBron played in Miami,

"YOU WANT TO BE A PART OF A TEAM THAT CAN GIVE THE BEST OPPORTUNITY TO WIN."

the Cavs suffered, never making the playoffs and finishing near the bottom of the Eastern Conference standings. As soon as LeBron returned in 2014, the Cavs started winning again. They reached the NBA Finals in four straight seasons, winning it all in 2016. Thanks to the Cavs picking up Kyrie Irving (through the 2011 NBA draft) and Kevin Love (via a trade in 2014), LeBron had the solid help he needed to make big things happen.

SEEK OUT THE BEST

When LeBron James joined the Los Angeles Lakers in 2018, he was one of a few veteran players on the team, but he was surrounded by young players that he could build up, like Kyle Kuzma, Lonzo Ball, Brandon Ingram, and Alex Caruso. He attempted to bring those players all the way, but

fell short of the playoffs after missing 30 games due to a groin injury. In 2019, LeBron helped recruit Anthony Davis to the Lakers. It helped that Davis was in LeBron's circle. He was represented by Klutch Sports, an agency started by James and his friend Rich Paul, one of The Four Horsemen. In 2020, the Los Angeles Lakers, led by Davis and LeBron, were on fire. They made quick work of the other postseason teams, going no more than five games in each of the first three rounds of the playoffs and beating the Miami Heat in the sixth game of the NBA Finals to win the championship.

After the Los Angeles Lakers made an early exit in the 2021 NBA playoffs, LeBron committed to rebooting his team's roster, once again recruiting players in an effort to surround

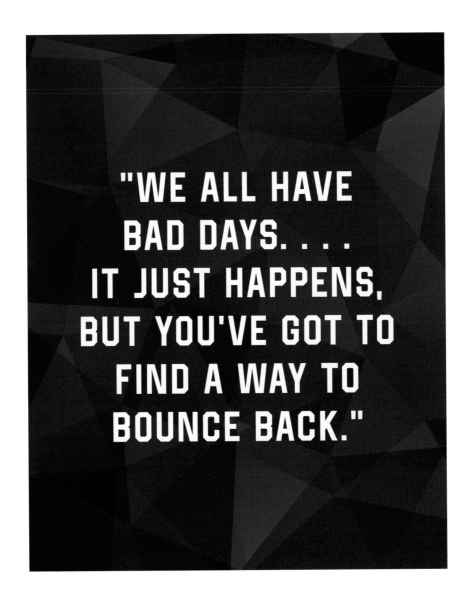

"WE ALL HAVE BAD DAYS. . . . IT JUST HAPPENS, BUT YOU'VE GOT TO FIND A WAY TO BOUNCE BACK."

SHOULDERING DREAMS

LeBron has been instrumental in capturing four NBA titles. He's helped make championship dreams come true for 54 other NBA players.

himself with greatness. By the time the 2021–22 season began, the Lakers, pushed heavily by and inspired by LeBron's vision, had assembled a team for the ages. Among the all-time greats on the team: LeBron, Davis, and additions DeAndre Jordan, Dwight Howard, Carmelo Anthony, and Russell Westbrook. Any one of those players could be a superstar on offense, but instead, LeBron persuaded them to put their egos aside in search of a common goal: to win another championship for the Los Angeles Lakers.

FAMILY FIRST

Like all of the old friends in his inner circle, LeBron's family keeps him grounded and focused on what matters most. His wife, Savannah, has known him since they were students at rival high schools and attended prom together. She was there for every stage of LeBron's spectacular rise to fame, from the day he was drafted to the day he was named to the NBA's 75th Anniversary Team, a team of the best players in the NBA's 75-year history. They were married in 2013 and have three children together. Their oldest son, LeBron James Jr., nicknamed Bronny, is a very talented ballplayer, and is poised to play for major college basketball programs. LeBron has said that he won't retire until he can play alongside his son in an NBA game, ideally on the same team: "I would

STAT ⚡ In winning his fourth championship title, LeBron became the first superstar to lead three different teams to rings.

"BASKETBALL IS MY PASSION. I LOVE IT. BUT MY FAMILY AND FRIENDS MEAN EVERYTHING TO ME."

do whatever it takes to play with my son for one year," he said in an interview with *The Athletic*. "It's not about the money at that point." As LeBron approaches 40, he's prepared to usher in the next generation of players, especially if that generation includes his son.

LIFE LESSONS FROM THE KING

- NO ONE GOES IT ALONE.
- CHOOSE YOUR TEAM CAREFULLY.
- TRUST OTHER PEOPLE TO HELP YOU.
- BE THE BRIDGE TO THE NEXT GENERATION.

FIGHT FOR WHAT'S RIGHT

LeBron James recognizes his position of influence and power, and that speaking up for injustice or speaking out against society's ills and troubles is part of his job as a public figure. It's a role that he takes very seriously. For LeBron, giving back, helping out, and amplifying the cries of the unheard is a privilege he's equipped to handle.

His overarching goal is to leave a legacy that extends beyond basketball and entertainment and makes a difference in real peoples' lives. While he's risen to the top of the sports world and become one of the richest and most famous people on the planet, he is forever reminding himself that he's "a kid from Akron" who grew up with very little. With a large chunk of the money he makes playing basketball and running his businesses, he brings quantifiable, dramatic change to the lives of people who grew up in situations similar to his, sometimes even in his hometown.

PINPOINT WHAT MATTERS TO YOU

One of LeBron's first moves after joining the NBA was to establish The LeBron James Family Foundation. Created in 2004, when he was only 19 years old, the foundation aimed to positively affect children and young adults, specifically in the Akron area, by providing educational opportunities and extracurricular learning and self-betterment programs.

The first event sponsored by the foundation was a bikeathon. As a kid, LeBron was lucky enough to have a bike, which gave him mobility and the chance to explore, travel, play, and learn. In an effort to extend that same freedom to the youth in his hometown, LeBron hosted an annual bikeathon where he joined the kids and families for a ride through Akron and provided each of them with a bike of their own.

As a result of his family's financial struggles and a lack of consistency in his life, LeBron missed more than 80 days in his fourth-grade year, leading to one of many substantial gaps in his education. LeBron wasn't alone in his struggle. In the areas of Akron where LeBron grew up, there's a strong connection between low-income households and high dropout rates. In 2011, he started working toward closing the gap, giving back to and aiming to improve the lives of his home community with his substantial financial resources.

For LeBron, being able to give back was one of the most satisfying elements of his celebrity. When in 2017 he opened a magnet school for kids in Akron, it was, in his words, "one of the greatest moments (if not the greatest)" of his life. Even set against the thrill of winning championships, giving underserved kids a leg up felt deeply satisfying.

Via The LeBron James Family Foundation, he helped launch I PROMISE, an initiative serving more than 1,000 economically disadvantaged and educationally lagging kids in the Akron school system. I PROMISE became a

"OUR VISION IS TO CREATE A PLACE FOR THE KIDS IN AKRON WHO NEED IT MOST."

full-fledged magnet institution, the I PROMISE School, in 2018. The foundation works with Akron Public Schools to identify children who have fallen a year or more behind in their studies and skill level, or are in danger of doing so: "If we get to them early enough," explains LeBron, "we can hopefully keep them on the right track to a bigger and brighter future for themselves and their families."

HOLD THE DOOR OPEN

The school expanded from third and fourth grade to two separate programs covering at-risk students in grades one through eight. LeBron was careful not to simply put a bandage on Akron's education system. He made sure that his foundation also addressed the key underlying causes behind kids'

poor grades or excessive absences. Recognizing the importance of education as well as stability, LeBron makes sure that I PROMISE takes a holistic approach to its hundreds of students, offering money for uniforms, bicycles, food for the entire family, transportation to and from school, and GED and job-placement services for its students' parents.

The LeBron James Family Foundation is also credited with the I PROMISE Network Scholarship, which offers free higher learning to those who meet the requirements. Akron Public Schools students who graduate with a grade point average of at least 3.0 are eligible for a full, four-year scholarship to the University of Akron, a scholarship funded in part by LeBron himself. It's estimated that at

"PEOPLE WILL HATE YOU, RATE YOU, SHAKE YOU, AND BREAK YOU. BUT HOW STRONG YOU STAND IS WHAT MAKES YOU."

INVEST IN KIDS

ESPN's 2010 special "The Decision," in which LeBron announced his move from the Cleveland Cavaliers to the Miami Heat, earned millions in advertising revenue. As producer, he coordinated with ESPN to donate $2.5 million of the proceeds to the Boys and Girls Clubs of America.

least 2,000 students who otherwise wouldn't have attended college will receive the chance to do so because of this program.

TELL YOUR STORY

LeBron has frequently and openly shared the story of his often-difficult childhood, including the experience of being raised by a single mother who experienced job and housing insecurity, the gaps in his education, and the family's financial struggles. It's a reminder to himself and to the world at large that he came from very humble origins, and that a lot of hard work and support made his dream come true. He sets himself up as an example that with enough determination, plus a strong community of dedicated supporters, almost anything is possible.

"THIS SKINNY KID FROM AKRON WHO MISSED 83 DAYS OF SCHOOL IN THE FOURTH GRADE HAD BIG DREAMS."

LEBRON ON DISPLAY

The LeBron James Family Foundation is working toward the opening of a LeBron James Museum in Akron. It will showcase, among other things, his size 15 basketball shoes. Proceeds from the museum will help fund the I PROMISE school and charity.

Being honest and authentic connects LeBron to his fans and turns his superhuman façade into something very normal and relatable. It also encourages us to act accordingly, accepting our own past and embracing the challenges ahead.

For accepting and using his role as a leader in professional sports for positive change, LeBron was awarded the NAACP's Jackie Robinson Sports Award in 2016 (the same year he donated $2.5 million to the Smithsonian National Museum of African American History and Culture to fund an exhibit on boxer and civil rights crusader Muhammad Ali). A year later, the NBA gave LeBron its J. Walter Kennedy Citizenship Award for "outstanding service and dedication to the community." But LeBron doesn't push for social change for the accolades. He does it because he passionately cares about the things to which he donates his money, time, and voice.

BE A VOICE FOR JUSTICE

LeBron James, as a Black man and one of the highest-profile members of the NBA, a league in which 80 percent of its athletes are Black, utilizes his celebrity influence and has been outspoken in his comments about the racially motivated, police-related deaths of multiple African Americans in the 2010s through the present.

In March 2012, LeBron and teammate Dwyane Wade organized a Miami Heat team photo in which everyone wore hooded sweatshirts and posted it to social media, a quiet but powerful statement against the

"I BELIEVE
IN ORDER FOR US
TO ULTIMATELY BE AS
GREAT AS WE CAN
BE AS A NATION
THAT ALL OF US HAVE
TO GO BACK INTO
OUR COMMUNITIES
AND LEND OUR HAND."

"OBVIOUSLY OUR SOCIETY NEEDS TO DO BETTER."

fatal shooting of a Black, hoodie-wearing Florida teenager named Trayvon Martin.

In November 2014, LeBron publicly decried the destruction of property in Ferguson, Missouri, over the ruling that the police officer who shot Black teenager Mike Brown in Ferguson would not face criminal charges. LeBron has said that this case in particular "hit home" for him. It was a small indication of a much larger, ongoing issue:

> *"It's not just one instance. It's not just Mike Brown or Trayvon Martin or anything that's going on in our society. I think it's much bigger than that."*

A few weeks later, before a game in New York City, LeBron (along with Kyrie Irving and several Brooklyn Nets players) wore a T-shirt bearing the message "I can't breathe" during warm-ups. It was a reference to the last words of Eric Garner, a 43-year-old Black man who died in 2014 after being placed in a chokehold by an NYPD officer. "It was a message to the family," explained LeBron, "that I'm sorry for their loss, sorry to his wife."

The 2016 ESPY Awards were held within weeks of two more police shootings of Black men, Alton Sterling in Louisiana and Philando Castile in Minnesota. LeBron took a few minutes out of the otherwise celebratory ceremony to acknowledge the deaths, and to reiterate that such hostile, violent, and racist activities could not continue. Alongside friends and colleagues Dwyane Wade, Carmelo Anthony, and Chris Paul, LeBron delivered a passionate speech about racism and gun violence:

"We all feel helpless and frustrated by the violence. We do. But that's not acceptable. It's time to look in the mirror and ask ourselves what are we doing to create change. It's not about being a role model. It's not about our responsibility to the tradition of activism. Let's use this moment as a call to action for all professional athletes to educate ourselves. It's for these issues. Speak up. Use our influence. And renounce all violence. And most importantly, go back to our communities, invest our time, our resources, help rebuild them, help strengthen them, help change them."

When in 2017, just ahead of the NBA Finals, a racial slur was spray-painted on the side of his Los Angeles home, LeBron turned it into an opportunity to show his fans and the public what it's like to be Black in America:

"No matter how much money you have, no matter how famous you are, no matter how many people admire you, being Black in America is tough. We got a long way to go for us as a society and for us as African Americans until we feel equal in America."

REFUSE TO BE SILENCED

LeBron made speaking his mind a habit, refusing to take the safe path of shying away from politics. After a 2018 interview in which LeBron openly voiced his thoughts on politics, the sitting president, and the racist graffiti, Laura Ingraham, a well-known Fox News commentator, announced on her

"I REPRESENT A MUCH BIGGER CALLING THAN JUST BASKETBALL."

show that she was not interested in his political point of view and advised him to just "shut up and dribble."

In response to the dismissive comment, LeBron took the high road and transformed the media moment into an opportunity to give people of color a voice. He went to work co-creating a 2018 documentary series for Showtime about politically minded NBA athletes called *Shut Up and Dribble*, repurposing the insult in the best way he could. He wasn't interested in defending himself from Ingraham's remarks, because he knew that they were just a symptom of a greater problem:

> *"I'm going to continue to do what I have to do to play this game that I love to play, but this is bigger than me playing the game of basketball."*

STAY ON MESSAGE

The NBA became a platform for political expression in 2020 and the years of unrest that followed. In the wake of the police-related deaths of George Floyd in Minneapolis and Breonna Taylor in Kentucky, the NBA added the words "Black Lives Matter" to courts and allowed social-justice messaging on the back of player jerseys for the remainder of the season.

In July 2020, after his first scrimmage before the NBA's post–COVID-19 shutdown restart, LeBron demonstrated that, at the end of the day, community, justice, and outreach are more important than basketball. Using his entire 14-minute interview with the press, LeBron spoke little of sports and instead focused on Breonna Taylor, racism, and police violence:

> *"We want the cops arrested who committed that crime. I know a lot of people are feeling the same. And us as the NBA, and us as the players, and me as one of the leaders of this league, I want her family to know and I want the state of Kentucky to know that we feel for it and we want justice. That's what it's all about. What's right is right and what's wrong is wrong. And this is a wrong situation that's going on in my eyes and in a lot of other eyes."*

"IT'S ABOUT BEING ABLE TO SHED LIGHT ON THINGS THAT ARE GOING ON IN OUR COMMUNITIES."

To combat such violence and to encourage change, LeBron teamed up with other athletes to launch More Than a Vote, an initiative committed to getting young Black people to participate in the American electoral process. "People in our community have been just lied to for so many years," said LeBron. "We have people that have had convictions in the past, that've been told they cannot vote because they got a conviction. That is voter suppression." While others kept silent on this issue and more, LeBron was making it a habit to stand up and say something.

He paid attention when the Black community needed him and intervened to become a vehicle for positive political change. Kelly Loeffler, an owner of the WNBA's Atlanta Dream, ran for a U.S. Senate seat in 2020, campaigning against the Black Lives Matter movement that had electrified the nation (and the NBA) that year. LeBron, a vocal supporter of Black Lives Matter and other programs that empower underserved communities, helped Renee Montgomery, a Black woman and WNBA player, form an investor group and purchase Loeffler's share of the team.

In August 2020, with his Los Angeles Lakers clearly on their way to winning an NBA title in the bubble, the Milwaukee Bucks boycotted a playoff game against the Orlando Magic after Jacob Blake, a Black man from Kenosha, Wisconsin, was shot seven times by a police officer. They refused to speak with the media until they issued a boycott, and the rest of the league refused to play for two days. They held an all-hands players meeting to decide if they wanted to stop the season entirely as a show of commitment to social justice. As the league's biggest star and biggest name, LeBron could have single-handedly shut down the league and the NBA bubble for the season if he'd wanted to.

After speaking with retired NBA superstar Michael Jordan and former President Barack Obama, LeBron helped NBA players find another way to make a difference. LeBron, already involved in nationwide drives to increase voter turnout in the African American community, teamed up with Michigan Secretary of State Jocelyn Benson to successfully urge the NBA to use its empty arenas as voting centers that upcoming fall, including the Lakers' home, the Staples Center. "Homecourt!" LeBron tweeted when the news dropped that his team's arena would serve Los Angeles–area voters.

EMBRACE THE MOMENT

LeBron and the vast majority of NBA players in the Orlando bubble decided against a boycott and stayed. In post-game interviews, LeBron continued to talk more about the Black Lives Matter movement and social justice than he did about

"WE AS A LEAGUE AND WE AS PLAYERS ARE STRONGER TOGETHER THAN SEPARATE."

THERE ARE NO WORDS

As part of its social justice initiative, the NBA authorized a list of messages that players could opt to print on their jerseys in 2020, including "I Can't Breathe," "Anti-Racist," and "Vote." LeBron's jersey didn't carry a slogan. "I don't need to have something on the back of my jersey for people to understand my mission or know what I'm about and what I'm here to do," he told reporters.

basketball. He also helped form a social justice coalition among players, coaches, and owners and negotiated with the NBA to produce and air ads during games to push greater voter access. "When you're trying to create change," he explained, "you can't lose sight of what the main thing is and why we came down here. We came down here for a mission."

LIFE LESSONS FROM THE KING

- **MAKE SOCIAL JUSTICE A PRIORITY.**

- **EDUCATE YOURSELF ON IMPORTANT TRUTHS, AND GET THE WORD OUT.**

- **SPEAK OUT FOR THOSE WHO CANNOT SPEAK FOR THEMSELVES, AND WORK TOWARD CHANGES THAT ARE DESPERATELY NEEDED.**

- **EMBRACE THE MOMENT AND YOUR INFLUENCE.**

"CHANGE ISN'T MADE SITTING ON THE SIDELINES."

I'M LEBRON JAMES

"Listen, for me I can't worry about what everybody say about me. I'm LeBron James from Akron, Ohio. From the inner city. I'm not even supposed to be here. That's enough. Every night I walk into the locker room, I see a No. 6 with *James* on the back. I'm blessed. So what everybody say about me off the court don't matter. I ain't got no worries."

—2013 MVP Award Speech

RESOURCES

MAGAZINES/WEBSITES/ NEWSPAPERS

"14 Examples of LeBron James' Incredible Work Ethic"
Business Insider, July 11, 2014

"35 Inspirational LeBron James Quotes on Success"
Awaken the Greatness Within, 2021

"Ahead of His Class: Ohio High School Junior LeBron James Is So Good That He's Already Being Mentioned as the Heir to Air Jordan"
Sports Illustrated, February 18, 2002

"Best LeBron James Quotes: Childhood, Basketball, Leadership, Success"
Nasty Dunk, October 2, 2020

"The Burden of Leadership, LeBron James"
Coaching Clipboard, June 7, 2016

"Cari Champion Responds to Laura Ingraham's Comments About LeBron James, Kevin Durant"
Sports Illustrated, February 22, 2018

"Could LeBron James Return to Cleveland Again? 'The Door's Not Closed on That,' He Says"
The Athletic, February 19, 2022

"Full Transcript of Lebron James Interview with Larry King"
New York Post, June 2, 2010

"How Good Was LeBron James in High School Basketball? We Take a Look at His High School Stats, Career and Highlights"
Sportskeeda, November 24, 2021

"How LeBron James Helped Renee Montgomery Buy the Atlanta Dream"
Yahoo! Sports, February 26, 2021

"Laura Ingraham Told LeBron James to Shut Up and Dribble; He Went to the Hoop"
NPR, February 19, 2018

"LeBron: I'm Coming Back to Cleveland"
Sports Illustrated, July 11, 2014

"LeBron James"
BasketballReference.com

LeBron James
Instagram (@KingJames)
February 19, 2014

LeBron James
Twitter (@KingJames)
August 29, 2020

"LeBron James"
USA Basketball, November 8, 2021

"LeBron and His Friends Are Telling Their Story for the First Time"
Andscape, November 19, 2018

"LeBron James and the Quote Heard Round the World"
The Nation, June 13, 2011

"LeBron James: Bigger Issues at Play"
ESPN, November 25, 2014

"LeBron James Chalk Toss: Why and When Did Lakers Superstar Begin His Pre-game Chalk Toss Ritual?"
The Sports Rush, October 13, 2021

"LeBron James' Decision: the Transcript"
ESPN, July 8, 2010

"LeBron James Declares for NBA Draft"
CBC Sports, April 25, 2003

"LeBron James Delivers Passionate Comments About Breonna Taylor and the Need for Change"
Sports Illustrated, July 23, 2020

"LeBron James Extends a Remarkable NBA MVP Streak in Getting a Lone Fifth-Place Vote"
Sportscasting, June 9, 2021

"LeBron James Family Foundation and Akron Public Schools Establish the I PROMISE School"
Andscape, April 18, 2017

"LeBron James Has Always Shown an Interest in Cinema" *Showbiz CheatSheet*, May 26, 2020

"LeBron James Is Embracing Playing Power Forward for the Cavaliers Like Never Before" *Cleveland Plain-Dealer*, March 5, 2016

"LeBron James Is Live in New York and Would Like to Host on Saturday Night Again Someday" *Cleveland Plain-Dealer*, February 21, 2015

"LeBron James Is Speaking Out When Too Many Are Silent" *USA Today*, December 9, 2014

"LeBron James Is Taking His 3-Point Game to Another Stratosphere" *Sportscasting,* January 4, 2021

"LeBron James' More Than a Vote Launches New Campaign to Defend Voting Rights" *CBS News*, March 5, 2021

"LeBron James' Net Worth Revealed —And Spoiler, He's Not a Billionaire" *Forbes*, August 8, 2021

"LeBron James on Work Ethic, Sustaining Longevity and Being a True Veteran" *Cleveland Plain-Dealer*, February 14, 2016

"LeBron James Reunites with St. Vincent–St. Mary's 'Fab Five' at I PROMISE School" *USA Today*, August 14, 2019

"LeBron James Says He Sees Himself with the Lakers for 'As Long as I Can Play'" *NBA.com*, February 26, 2022

"LeBron James Says He 'Would Have Made' NFL Team If He Tried Out During 2011 Lockout" *NFL.com*, February 16, 2021

"LeBron James Scraps Written Speech, Delivers Heartfelt Message to Honor Kobe Bryant During Lakers Ceremony" *CBS News*, February 2, 2020

"LeBron James' Secret to Ignoring Lakers Haters: 'Drink Wine or Tequila Every Night'" *Washington Times*, March 22, 2022

"LeBron James Seemingly Calls Out Players Who Practice Things They Won't Use in Games: 'Annoys Me a Tad'"
Fadeaway World, September 18, 2021

"LeBron James' Troubled Ex-Stepfather Eddie Jackson Arrested for DUI in Miami Beach"
Miami New Times, February 12, 2014

"LeBron James Voices Support for Bucks NBA Boycott: 'We Demand Change'"
The Hill, August 26, 2020

"LeBron James Wants to Be Remembered as 'One of the Most Unselfish Players Ever'"
USA Today, November 8, 2017

"LeBron Learned His Lessons From Riley—and Wants to Show Some This Finals"
South Florida Sun-Sentinel, September 29, 2020

"LeBron Takes on 'Burden of Leading'"
ESPN, November 19, 2014

"LeBron Won't Wear Social Justice Message on Lakers Jersey"
The Associated Press, July 11, 2020

"LeBron's 'More Than a Vote' Pushing for Arenas to Be Voting Sites"
USA Today, July 1, 2020

"LeGM at the Table? 5 Times LeBron James Tried to Personally Recruit Players in the NBA"
Sportskeeda, September 6, 2021

"Life Lessons from a Champion: LeBron James"
Success Media Solutions, 2019

"Los Angeles Lakers' LeBron James Oldest Player Ever to Post 30-Point Triple-double"
ESPN, December 12, 2021

"Lost Stories of LeBron, Part 1"
ESPN the Magazine, October 17, 2013

"Mag.Commentary"
ESPN the Magazine, December 19, 2002

"Ranking LeBron James' Seven NBA Head Coaches over the Course of His Career"
USA Today, July 5, 2018

"'She's My Champion': LeBron James Writes Tribute to His Single Mom." *Today*, January 12, 2014

"Spring Hill, No. 602: For LeBron James and Others, a Place to Dream" *The Athletic,* February 16, 2022

"Stepping Outside the Comfort Zone, LeBron James" *Coaching Clipboard*, August 31, 2015

"Three Weeks in Crazyville" *GQ,* August 16, 2010

"What LeBron James Can Teach Us About Greatness" *Wealthy Gorilla*, May 3, 2021

"Where LeBron James Stands When We Talk About Advanced Stats: Player Efficiency, Win Share, Plus-Minus, Value Over Replacement" *Fadeaway World,* October 1, 2021

"'We Know It's Bigger Than Us.' LeBron James Expands on Why He Feels Compelled to Speak on Social Issues After Criticism from Laura Ingraham" *Business Insider,* February 17, 2018

BOOKS

LeBron, Inc.: The Making of a Billion-Dollar Athlete, by Brian Windhorst

LeBron James, by Valerie Bodden

LeBron James, by Ryan Nagelhout

LeBron James, by Heather E. Schwartz

LeBron James: The Life, Lessons, and Rules for Success, published by Influential Individuals

LeBron's Dream Team: How Five Friends Made History, by Buzz Bissinger and LeBron James

*The Playbook: 52 Rules to Aim, Shoot, and Score in This Game Called Lif*e, by Kwame Alexander

Return of the King: LeBron James, the Cleveland Cavaliers, and the Greatest Comeback in NBA History, by Brian Windhorst and Dave McMenamin

"THE GAME
OF BASKETBALL
MEANS EVERYTHING.
THIS IS LOVE."